Wander Lust

A sassy, sexy memoir of my journey from the known to the wild unknown

BETHANY PLATANELLA

CONTENTS

To my parents.
Thank you for always letting me run free.

PREFACE

I watch Sam cry as he steps into the car, and my heart breaks. It doesn't immediately occur to me that this is the last time I'll ever see this handsome and loving man as my official boyfriend. Both of us knowing, but not saying, what is truly happening. Our years together start to slip into a filing cabinet of past lives as his car pulls away.

I grab the handle of my oversized suitcase, lower my sunglasses to mask puffy, red eyes, and set out to find my mother in this chaotic, loud, and bustling airport. We are going to Barcelona today, a city that I have never been to but have chosen as my new home for the next three months, … which will turn into five, which will turn into fourteen, which turn into… well, you get the picture.

I see her, small and compact, shining eyes filled with excitement and anticipation for what's to come. My mother has always been a supporter of my dreams, so six months ago when I made the decision to save money, quit my job, move out of my apartment, and leave my boyfriend and life in exchange for the unknown in Spain, she did not hesitate to say, "Do it."

But before I get on the plane, let me backtrack.

How did I get here? $8,000, one giant suitcase, a Spanish dictionary, and a round-trip ticket to Barcelona. When the idea to skip across the pond surfaced, I began saving money to an obsessive degree, poring through every book and article available to aid me in my international relocation.

Why? There are several reasons, really, all of which seemed to culminate into one pressing, passionate need to get out of the United States and get myself to Europe.

Reason #1: Exploration

I'd been chattering away about traveling since I could talk. At five, I wanted to go to Colorado. At eight, I wanted to go to Egypt in hot pursuit of the elusive mysteries of King Tut and the Pyramids. At age ten, I spent a good (and embarrassing) year or more of my life speaking in a paltry British accent, hoping it would magically relocate me to a place and period of time where tea and biscuits, high-waisted, muslin dresses and elegant white gloves reigned supreme. So it was only natural that by the age of twenty-four, when my brand-new adult life proved slightly boring and highly predictable, I would exchange it for a temporary escapade in sunny, seductive Spain.

Reason #2: A gripping fear of monotony

My job in the city paid well. Too well, honestly, for the mindless work I was doing. Every day I took four flights of stairs to my gray cubicle, welcoming any form of exercise that might assist in burning off the excess of calories I was consuming in craft beer and crappy food. I would sit down in this energy-sucking box and putz around online for a good hour or so before starting anything productive. Myspace, national and local news, personal email - anything was a viable distraction to tackling the truly mundane tasks expected of me as a Marketing Assistant to a group of architects. It was during one of these hours of procrastinating that my inspiration to leave was ignited. Google Mail at the time had a fantastic application called "One Thousand Places to See Before You Die." Every time I signed into my email, a new, exotic destination would pop up on my screen. The Great Wall of China. The Amalfi Coast. Copacabana Beach. Norwegian Fjords. The pictures mesmerized me. I could almost feel sharp, icy gusts of wind dancing off Neva Bay in a chilly St. Petersburg as my eyes devoured pictures of Russia.

And then, something snapped inside of me. Looking at pictures wasn't enough. I needed to explore, and I knew exactly who to drag along with

me. Sam, my cohabitation partner, my best friend, my rock. Sam and I were going on 5 years together and were still as inseparable as we were when we started. He was tall, dark, handsome, smart, funny, personable, and happy. We were the couple that every couple strived to be, always laughing and affectionate, just the right amount of dramatic and jealous. In so many ways, he was perfect…
for someone else.

"Sam," I called out breathlessly as I stumbled into our drafty apartment with beautiful floor to ceiling windows that never quite shut all the way. Our typical city apartment was in a converted factory that had concrete floors, keeping the temperature frosty throughout most of the year. I shivered and called out again, a little louder this time as Sam was a bit distracted by ESPN's coverage of his favorite baseball team.

"Sam! What do you think about going away for a while? Traveling a bit? What do you think? Italy? China? Brazil?" My mind was racing with possibilities, hiking through the Alps in Switzerland, sampling fresh sushi in bustling Japanese markets, a wild safari adventure in Kenya. Distant China called to me, there was something so exotic about Asia…

Sam interrupted my thought stream, "I don't know. I would have to think about it, and see what vacation time I have, when to go, and how much money we can spend. Can we talk about it another time?" He shot me a smile and settled back into his sports bubble.

Another time? Really?

I literally couldn't think of a more exciting topic than travel. I wanted to talk about it and think about it and breathe it *all* the time. Why would he want to talk about it *later*? As I marveled at his brushoff, I considered the points he'd raised. He wanted to check on his vacation time. Okay, this was logical. I guess, as one of his real estate firm's top employees, he would need permission to take off. Justified. He also wanted to research when to go. Why? I wanted to go ASAP. Finally, he wanted to see how much money we could spend. What for? Couldn't we just pick a location and figure it out from there? These felt like excuses from the mouth of a person who wasn't interested in going anywhere. I pressed him a bit more.

"Um, sure, when would you like to talk about it?" In five minutes? Over dinner? Before bed? I stood there, wide-eyed with anticipation.

"I don't know babe, later. Are you hungry?"

My eyes rolled involuntarily. I wanted to snub him of the luxury of having me as a dinner mate out of spite. Unfortunately, my empty stomach outweighed my obstinacy.

Reason #3: Living in the wrong country

The USA is beautiful. It is convenient, successful, strong, logical. Americans work hard, play harder. But, through the working, the playing, the money, and time spent, life seems to get away from us. How many times do we actually sit down to enjoy our overpriced and over-sugared Frappuccino from Starbucks? Only on Saturdays? Why is our leisure time, our time to really appreciate the world, to unwind and relax, regulated to one or two weeks a year? Why must we feel guilty to sit in a cafe for hours, reading, watching, smelling, listening, feeling? And why, most importantly, can most other countries appreciate life to an extent that we cannot?

I needed answers that I couldn't find here. The desire for material objects surrounded me daily, but I couldn't relate. I didn't want these things. $5,000 on a couch … are you kidding me? That's an entire month in Thailand with plane fare included! That's more than a week of hopping around the Greek Islands, staying in their finest hotels. I don't care what piece of furniture I'm sitting on as long as I can talk about my authentic experience in a steamy Turkish Hammam while I'm sitting on it. My ideas of fulfillment differed greatly from most people around me, and so I had to find where the like-minded thinkers resided.

With those three reasons, I set out on a 43,000-mile journey to find my truth while collecting a fabulous kaleidoscope of experiences: dancing the night away on the shores of the Iberian peninsula, living with ten 20-somethings from all over the world in a small 3-room flat in Barcelona, sailing the seas as an English-speaking hostess and crewmember of a few

Italian cruise ships, falling in love with more than my fair share of foreign men, and starting beautiful, emotional friendships that would continue well into my later years. These experiences chipped and molded me to reveal the adventurous, confident, confused, sexy, and happy self that I never knew could exist.

Settling into my new room. Barcelona, 2009.

PORT I
BARCELONA

1

MARIO

Mario must be the man who is coming to fix the wardrobe, though it doesn't look like it needs to be fixed. I hope he's cute in a scruffy way, with tanned skin and tousled hair, wide shoulders and strong arms. That's how I imagine a Catalán carpenter to look. Slightly sweaty, fingernails stained by the manly labor required to perfect that dresser. I'll stand behind him, watching him work. When he's completed the task, he'll turn around, look deep into my eyes, and in a fury of intoxicating desire, he'll lift me up in those muscular arms and…

"BAH-LAY?"

I'm rudely snapped out of my delicious daydream by Maria, the woman currently standing in front of me. Why does she keep saying bah-lay? What does that even mean?

I stand, perplexed, mom by my side, struggling to understand and translate what Maria is saying. More accurately, trying to translate the conversation that Maria is having with herself, because in between drags of cigarettes, she is rattling on a mile a minute and using words I have never learned in my ten years of Spanish class. I take it from context clues that this wardrobe in front of us is going to be mine, it needs to be fixed by Mario, and bah-lay must be a Catalán phrase for *"Do you understand?"*.

"Si, si, entiendo," I say. But, I, clearly, do not *entiendo.* It takes me a while to figure out that my handsome, scruffy and strong carpenter, Mario, is actually *armario*, as in armoire or the closet where I have been instructed to unpack my things. The closet that needs no repairs whatsoever. And bah-lay? Bah-lay is actually, *vale.* Or the Spanish from Spain version of "okay."

Vale, I am getting it now.

Maria, better known as our "house mom," is the owner of the apartment where I will be staying. She's in her late forties with badly dyed blonde hair, tanned, slightly leathery skin, and a smoker's cough that would shock Allen Carr. (Alan Carr, the author of the very successful Alan Carr's *Easy Way to Stop Smoking*, claimed to have smoked 100 cigarettes a day at the peak of his addiction.) Maria's eyes are sunken, but beneath their exterior there is a certain twinkle to them. She is very beautiful, or was, a beauty tainted by years of nicotine, depression, eating disorders, and probably drugs. A past-time party girl, Maria now rents out her gorgeous, antique, 3-bedroom flat to as many Spanish Language students as will fit in it.

We continue to the kitchen. Maria opens the refrigerator, located directly to the left of the entrance. Inside are shelves that have been labeled. "Morimoyo," "Jenni," "Natasha," "Bobby," "Chaune," and "Marita." Milk, cheese, eggs, orange soda, a carrot or two, potatoes, tomatoes, yogurt. Maria then takes us a few steps to the right to reveal the cabinets, which are stocked with giant bottles of olive oil, sugar, instant coffee, canned corn, and rice. I gather that we each have our own sections of the kitchen to keep our food items. Olive oil, sugar, paper towels, dish soap, and other random cleaning supplies are to be equally funded by the housemates with weekly payments to be deposited in a big, rusty tin can placed on the countertop. As renters, we are responsible for cleaning and maintaining the kitchen in an orderly manner.

A wooden table juts out from the wall behind me. The table is occupied by four suspicious and expectant eyes, each set analyzing my reaction to this new life. I gaze upon two girls in their early twenties. The dark-haired one, Natasha, dives right into an explosive series of blunt questions and observations.

"Are you American?" Natasha is stunning. Her hair is thick and dark, her huge hazel eyes are framed by insanely (natural!) long eyelashes, and her skin is a flawless shade of caramel. She is munching on a plate of bread, cheese, and olives as pasta cooks on the stove.

"Yes," I say, meekly.

"Yah, we thought so. We looked at the tag on your suitcase. You brought so much stuff we knew you HAD to be American."

My mother and I mutually perk up at the word "suitcase." My luggage was lost in our short connection at the Madrid Barajas airport. For the last five days, I've fought with the airline company in Spanglish, trying to track down my suitcase. This ordeal leads to one of my first introductions to Spanish culture: the Spanish will say anything to get you off the phone. "Arrive two hours." AKA, five days later -- the suitcase has apparently arrived and serves as an apt communicator of my cultural background.

I turn to my mother, mouth slightly ajar. Before I have the chance to speak, Natasha pipes in again.

"Your suitcase is in the dining room. It arrived here yesterday. I didn't know they made luggage so big. How long are you staying here? What room are you in?"

Her incessant questioning is making my head spin, and I am finding it hard to respond. I manage to mumble answers to her gratification.

"Why did you bring so much if you are only here for three months? Are you staying in the back room? You have a window. But you can hear the girl who is sleeping in the next room, the walls are thin. I'm

Natasha, I'm from the Netherlands. This is Jenni. She is also from the Netherlands, but from a different city. What city are you from? Are you hungry? Tonight we are having a house *cena* to welcome you. Maria will cook tortilla, *pan con tomate*, chicken, and rice. Do you eat chicken?"

First introduction to Dutch culture: The Dutch never stop talking.

Suddenly, a closet door opens in the hallway. (Please re-read that. A closet door.) Out steps a small Asian man who appears to be in his mid-thirties. He makes his way to the kitchen. I sneak a peek inside the closet before he shuts the door behind him. No windows, lots of shelves, lots of guitars.

"Hola, yo soy Morimoyo. Bienvenida a nuestra casa."

His voice is like velvet, soft and buttery with melodic undertones. Each syllable is pronounced with precision. Morimoyo is from Kyoto, Japan, he plays and makes guitars and works at a music shop in Barrio Gótico. He has a Catalán girlfriend, speaks absolutely no English, and lives in a converted closet.

"No necesitan mucho espacio, los japoneses!" Japanese don't need a lot of space, laughs Maria, evidently her justification for taking his hard-earned rent money every month in exchange for a room no bigger than a bathroom stall. I contemplate this scenario and quickly decide that I don't have the energy for it now.

Feeling a bit overwhelmed, I turn to my mother once again. "Shall we unpack my things and explore a little before dinner?" She smiles sweetly and we shuffle down the hall toward my new room.

My room is more accurately a section of a normal-sized bedroom which has now been divided into two by a thin slice of sheetrock that doesn't quite reach the ceiling. On the other side of this sheetrock is another bedroom, which just about fits a bed and a small desk. Sheetrock doesn't do much in the way of soundproofing, so I can hear every move my neighbor makes and vice versa. My section of the room is long and thin but large enough to fit a desk, a wardrobe, a beautiful antique painting of a young girl with long blonde hair in a white dress, and a magnificent window framed by hunter green shutters from which I am specifically NOT allowed to hang laundry. (Dryers, on the whole, do not exist.) I feel almost guilty that I landed what is presumably the master suite. My mother senses my confusion and quickly reminds me to just be grateful.

As we unpack, I start to feel tingly. I am happy. More than happy. I am ecstatic, elated, insatiable. I want to know every corner of this city, every person, every style, every restaurant, market, bar, neighborhood, park. I want everything, all at once.

Mom and I finish unpacking feverishly and set out together for a long afternoon of exploration and learning. We walk for miles, taking pictures, drinking multiple cafés con leche, watching people go to and from work, learning the color-coded metro system. It is the first time she and I have traveled together, and we get along well. Too well, in fact, so that sharp pangs of melancholy dive through my gut when I think about her leaving. I try to remain appreciative for the time we have together.

Exhausted after hours of exploration, we return to my new home to find new faces scrambling about the dining room and kitchen, carrying platters of toasted bread with tomatoes, cheese, olives, tuna salad with corn, chicken and rice. Under a majestic chandelier is a long rectangular dining room table with wine bottles, both red and white, spread throughout. Metal trays clang and the clicking sound of lighters is almost constant. The house smells of olive oil and cigarettes, a smell that will permeate my nostrils for the majority of my stint in Europe.

As we start settling into chairs around the table, I can't help but notice two interesting additions to the group. Maria notices my curiosity because she immediately proceeds to introduce the boys as Bobby and Chaune. The two are from Turkey and are apparently a package deal. Chaune has icy blue eyes and long, black eyelashes that naturally curl at the ends. He is muscular and slim with a well-defined jaw and high cheekbones. He will surely be one of the sexiest men to walk the earth as he ages. Bobby is also very handsome, but in a boyish way. He is dark and scruffy with broad shoulders, a bit of a pot belly and a happy, slightly crooked smile. He is aggressively flirtatious with me, not phased at all by the fact that I am seated next to my mother.

As the evening progresses, we all get drunk except for Maria. Maria only has half a glass of wine and about five cigarettes. Until this point, it seems that Spaniards don't drink as much as I thought they would. They drink with lunch, yes, with dinner, yes. However, the quantity consumed over an entire meal is nowhere near the quantity I normally consume before the meal even begins. I contemplate this for a brief moment, wondering if I have the ability to be that kind of person, when I feel my mother rise to help Maria in the kitchen.

Bobby, the house flirt, slides into her empty chair. He leans one elbow on the table and faces me directly. "Hi," he smiles.

"Hi," I reply.

We both blush, my cheeks surely reddened dramatically further by copious amounts of wine.

"Tell me about you," he says. His charming Turkish demeanor captivates me, and his gaze makes me feel like the only woman in the room.

And so begins the lifelong lesson in the ways of foreign men.

2
THE GIRLS

"I pressed the button already. Wait a few minutes, you know it takes a while!"

Natasha is suffering through an ice-cold shower, a common morning ritual we all must face when getting ready for school. The hot water heater, which turns off frequently and at the most inopportune times, is in the kitchen. If you are in the shower when the heater turns off, you will be hit by a continuous blast of frigid water that can only be remedied by jumping out and shrieking in agony until someone pushes the heater button. If no one responds, you are out of luck and must finish quickly under the cascade of freezing liquid. To top it off, not only are there just two bathrooms in this house of eleven students (one for three boys, the other for eight girls), but the bathrooms are divided by a frosted glass window. A relatively see-through divider that perfectly highlights the contours of your naked and shivering silhouette to whoever might be on the other side.

I sit down at the kitchen table next to Jenni. She is eating yogurt with kiwi like she does every morning. I start preparing my own breakfast of fruit and yogurt as the tea kettle starts rattling, indicating the water is ready to pour into my instant coffee. While many may grimace at the idea of instant coffee, I come to love it. The particular scent of it, the bitter taste, the grainy texture when it doesn't dissolve all the way…even today, a sip of instant coffee gleefully transports me back to this kitchen and to my friendship with Jenni.

Jenni is important to me. She is my support system, and I am hers. We think the same, we eat the same, we even like the same things, with the fortunate exception of men. We clicked almost instantly and have since done most everything as a unit. The major difference? Jenni is a hypochondriac. Like, total.

"I am so worried. My eye has not stopped stinging for four days now. I hope it isn't an infection, I don't want to be…what is the word in English when a person cannot see?"

I start to murmur the word she is looking for, *blind*, though her monologue overtakes my whisper.

"Blind! I don't want to be blind. Maybe later I will go to the doctor." Clearly pained, Jenni sighs.

Her health problems cover the gamut of body parts. Each day is something new, or something old is new again. Rashes, infections, fatigue, cuts and bruises that won't heal, fainting spells. On anyone else, this trait would drive me up a wall. With Jenni, it only makes me love her more.

"Can't you just put some eye drops in it? Or go to the pharmacy?" I reply, stifling my laughter so as to not make her feel worse or bring upon her yet another ailment.

"I am using eye drops all day! Nothing is working. Can you see anything in my eyeball? A scrape?"

Nothing. Looks perfectly fine to me. "No, honey, I don't see anything. I'll stop at the pharmacy with you after class."

We finish our breakfast, smoke a cigarette, wait for most of the group to meet at the door and make our way to the metro station. Red line, Urquinaona. (Try pronouncing that three times fast.) As usual, the Turkish boys won't make it to class; they were up late drinking gin and beer. And Morimoyo has to work. We girls squeeze our way onto a packed train car for the daily schlep to Spanish class. We speak English the entire way there.

To be perfectly honest, opportunities to speak Spanish in Barcelona are much fewer and farther between than I ever could have imagined. There are only two places for me to use my paltry language skills: in class and at the Vodafone store, which I have to frequent on a weekly basis to top up my cell phone credit. It feels both good and scary to enter one of the only public places in which Spanish is expected of me. No matter that I repeat the same exact phrase every time I go in there, the fact is I speak the language AND am understood! The remainder of my days and nights is spent frolicking with an international group of students, each of whom speaks nearly perfect English and doesn't care to converse in stumbling Spanish.

"What shall we do this weekend? Does anyone want to go to Shoko? I met a guy. He can put us on the list so we don't have to wait in line." Natasha is our go-to when it comes to club promoters.

But as glamorous as it sounds, I have other, much more stimulating plans. "I'm not going to be here this weekend. I'm leaving tomorrow for Tel-Aviv."

Rewind one year. My now ex-boyfriend goes on a trip to Vegas with his friends. So, what does any normal girlfriend do? She grabs her best girlfriend and goes to Miami! Nothing says "haha" better than a long weekend of drinks, sun, clubs, and innocent flirtation with beautiful, foreign men. Unless one of those beautiful, foreign men is a bit more intriguing than he should be, and you stay in touch with said beautiful, foreign man, until you are delightfully single enough to visit him in his hometown of Tel Aviv.

"You're going to Israel?? Are you sure you want to do that?" shrieks Marita. Marita is like a delicate

Chinese doll, one who defied her family's professional expectations and blasted off to Barcelona after college. As adventurous as she is, her conservative nature shocks me at times.

"Have you seen the guy I'm visiting?" A vision of Ari flashes through my mind. Long, dark hair, tanned, muscular build, deep, sultry eyes framed by curled eyelashes. If ever there were an Israeli clone of Johnny Depp in his youth, Ari is it. "Yes, I'm sure."

Since booking the ticket to Tel Aviv, I'm a mixed bag of emotions. This is a guy I spent a platonic weekend with more than a year ago but continue to think about nearly every weekend. And while most people would be anxious about the political situation in Israel (my parents will have no idea of my trip until after my return), I am more anxious about what to wear and how to properly introduce myself to his Hebrew-speaking mother. Politics be damned, I have bigger fish to fry, like making this hunk of handsome fall uncontrollably in love with me.

"That's right! Tonight is your Bon Voyage! Well, then, we should go to Dos Rosas. The cute bartender works on Thursdays." Jenni and her great ideas.

Dos Rosas is the spot for expats from all over the world. Arguably mixing the best mojitos in the city at an extremely affordable price, the walls are painted a deep red, and the bathrooms are wallpapered with ripped pages from decades-old porn magazines. It is dark and sexy like the Thursday night bartender who has a major crush on Jenni. The music is loud and trendy, and we can fashionably smoke as many ciga-rettes inside as our lungs allow with no complaints. To top it off, after one too many mojitos and the inevitable free shot or two, we can stumble into any nearby kebab shop on the way home to stave off the next morning's hangover. This is Catalunya, after all.

"Sounds good. So, after class let's stop at the phar-macy before siesta. Then we can have lunch at home, and then go to the beach. Dos Rosas around 9?" I look around at the group. Everyone nods in agreement.

We split for class, each girl stepping into her ap-propriately leveled classroom with dictionaries in tow. I smile when I think that in a mere 24 hours, I will be on my way to Israel.

3
THE ISRAELI INCIDENT

I *knew* I should have gone home after Dos Rosas. But there is something about those mojitos and chatty Dutch girls that can convince anyone to head to a club or the disco "just for one hour." It's *never* just one hour!

My house mom is fluttering up and down the hallway, smoking and rambling on in Spanish about my questionable decision to go to the Middle East. *Yes, I know it isn't the most stable of countries. Yes, I will send you a message when I get there.* But can someone just help me decide which wine to bring for his family?

I am running very late, I have a major hangover, and I do not look nearly as fresh and beautiful as

I had hoped to look on the day I am set to reunite with this Middle Eastern god. I throw what I have left to pack in a small suitcase and start to run to the door.

"Adios! Hasta martes!" The heavy door slams behind me as I agonizingly make my way down four flights of spiral staircase with my head spinning from leftover rum and nerves. Where is my Metro pass? Why is it never in the same spot I left it?

After digging around in my overstuffed bag and finally locating my Metro pass, I admit to myself that my only savior at this point is some coffee. The only coffee shop inside the Metro station is shamefully a Dunkin Donuts, so American. The thought of holding a cup with the logo pains me, but what can I do? I pull out one euro and head to the counter. "Un café con leche, por favor. Pequeño."

Everything in Europe is small. Okay not everything, but many things are small in a way that makes you really appreciate them. Coffee is a great example. A small coffee with milk in the United States holds a minimum of 10oz. A small coffee with milk in the Barcelona Metro station holds about 2oz. But the flavor in those 2oz. is enormous. Supersized soda? Forget it. You take your Coca Cola in a can or a bottle that maxes out at 10oz. The satisfaction is in the quality, not quantity. It's actually a great way to live life. Less fattening, too.

The cashier hands me my small café, and that's when I hear it -- the train whizzing by. *Damn, I missed it. I'll have to wait another 10 minutes at least, not that I really have that much time to spare. Oh well, all part of the adventure.*

I pay and head to the tracks, not knowing in the least the true adventure that awaits me.

"Can I ask you a few questions? Do you prefer to speak English or Spanish?" The gorgeous AirMiddleEast check-in woman smiles politely as I set my bag down on the scale.

"English is better for me." While I do thoroughly feel I'm on the verge of a breakthrough with my Spanish language skills, my lingering hangover and excitement to travel somewhere so alluring influences my decision to resort to English.

"Okay. So, what are you doing here in Barcelona?"

Hmm. By "questions" I thought she meant about my luggage, not my personal decision-making process and my inner demons. I decide to forgo the whole story of why I'm actually here and instead opt for the easy way out.

"I'm studying Spanish at a language school."

"Wonderful! Do you have a visa then?"

"No, I'm here for less than three months so I don't need a visa," I reply.

"What school are you going to?"

"Just a language school, it's not a university or anything."

"Oh. So what brings you to Israel?" she asks.

"I'm visiting a friend."

"How do you know this...friend?"

Did she just mock me? She definitely furrowed her brow when she said friend.

"I met him in Miami," I answer.

"Ohhh, Miami, very beautiful. So why are you visiting him?"

Okay this is none of her business. Why am I flying to a shaky, Middle Eastern war zone to visit a man? Do I HAVE to say this out loud?

"Because we are friends, and I like to travel."

"Is this relationship romantic?" she asks.

I certainly hope so. Wait a minute. Where is she going with this?

"I don't see how that question is relevant."

"Alright, well, what do his parents do?" she continues.

"His dad owns a business, and I think his mom is a teacher."

"What kind of business does his father own?"

Seriously?

"I'm sorry but I have no idea. And I don't think these questions are necessary for me to board this plane," I say.

"You know, each time we go to your country, we must answer many more questions than this."

Ah-ha! The bell goes off. I scan the crowd. I am the only blonde woman in a sea of dark, intense men. Why would I be going to Israel alone, on a Friday?

The beautiful Airline check-in girl continues. "I'm very sorry, but we are going to have to ask you some more questions. Could you follow me? We cannot hold up the line."

Panic sets in. *What is going on? Am I a target of some sort? Do I have any hash joints in my pockets that I've forgotten about?*

"N-n-no, no, I would rather stay, forget it, I am not going."

Her soothing voice hypnotizes me. "Do not wooohhhrry! Everything will be fine. Tel Aviv is a beautiful city, you will see. Just like Miami. We just first need to ask you some more questions."

I let her guide me to a tiny room behind the desk. She sits me down and takes my bag. Two extremely tall and very good-looking policemen enter what I begin to realize is an interrogation room. The door shuts.

I start freaking out. My lip starts to quiver, and my hands are trembling. Sweat is trickling down my temples as I fidget in my seat. *Don't leave me, beautiful check in girl. Don't leave me here, alone, with these men.*

"So." Handsome Policeman #1 sits in front of me. I jump a little. "You do not have to be scared. Why are you going to Israel?"

I explain myself. Again. My mouth is moving, and words are coming out, but terror is blocking my mind from comprehending the situation. Policeman #2 takes my bag.

"We must look through your things." As #2 shuffles through my clothes, #1 asks me more questions.

"Do you have a camera, telephone, iPod, laptop, or anything else electronic with you?"

"Yes, I have a camera, mobile phone, and an iPod."

"Take them out."

Policeman #1 proceeds to look through my text messages, my photos, and my music. My feelings are changing from ones of fear to infuriation. *Don't fight with him. This is not a situation that your occasional snappy attitude can fix.* The two men mumble to each other in Hebrew. *Really glad I've been wasting time with Spanish classes the past few weeks.*

"Okay, one more thing. Fatima needs to pat you down. You will have to remove your pants."

Remove my what?! Something snaps and angry words tumble from the core of my gut. I don't know what I'm saying anymore. I am yelling and crying and reaching for my bag to leave. Then Fatima's hypnotic voice steps in once again.

"Noooo, nooo, it is ohhhkaaay. Only you have to do like this!" She unbuttons the top of her pants to expose a lacey set of panties. In some alternate universe, this could actually be a scene out of SNL or a satire of some kind. However, at the moment, it is far from funny.

"No. Absolutely not," I protest.

"So we can go to the bathroom and you will have to change out of your jeans so we can scan you. The buttons will react to the scanner."

At the same time that Fatima explains the buttons and scanner, Policeman #2 hands me a pair of black leggings from my bag.

"You can change into these," he says.

How did he find these at such an opportune time?

Why did I even pack them? Are there camera crews anywhere? Is this Candid Camera? Or maybe a filming of the Twilight Zone? More importantly, why am I following these directions? Fatima and I head to the bathroom. I change into my leggings, fully aware that my perfect, introductory outfit that took five hours and my flat mates' help to settle on is now ruined. Fatima takes my jeans, soothing me with descriptions of gorgeous Israeli beaches and pumping nightclubs. I pass the scan. We return to the tiny questioning room where Policeman #1 is waiting for me. Feeling calmer now, I have a good look at his face. *Wow, he really is handsome.*

"Are you okay? I am so sorry to scare you this way. It is a procedure. Come with me and I will take you to the plane," he says.

I follow #1, who personally escorts me all the way to my window seat in row 15. "Can I get you anything else? Are you sure you are okay now? I don't want for you to be scared. You will have a wonderful time in Israel. Let me get a drink for you. Water? Coca cola?"

Water. Please. Now.

He leaves, and the plane takes off. I settle into my seat, slowing down my beating heart with breathing exercises.

"Hummus?"

I turn to see another breathtakingly beautiful woman with a lunch cart and a big smile. "Yes, please."

"Here you are! Hummus?" She continues to the next row.

I eat my well-deserved lunch of hummus, pita, rice and vegetables as I drift into a

daydream about what's to come. Funny how short one's memory can be when Israel is on the horizon.

4

CAN YOU TELL I'M
NOT FROM HERE?

This must be what it feels like to have brain surgery. I have absolutely no understanding of this language or this culture, and I am so completely out of my element that I have no idea how to act, rendering me not much different than a stone statue.

"Don't woohhrryy honey, every-wohn speaks English."

Ari's voice is so sexy, but he is full of shit. Everyone does NOT speak English, and even if they do, I feel like an asshole for not speaking a word of Hebrew. If only I could bring a flask everywhere we go, this would be easier. But *no*. The Israeli drinking culture is massively different from my own, as well as the Dutch and Swedish cultures with which I have been spending time. Alcohol is not used as a social crutch here, and for me to do so would just make me more of an alien.

"Today, we have no time for rest. My friend is having a party at his house, we can only change clothes and go right away," he says.

It's my second full day here, and we are coming from Masada, a desert plateau located above the Dead Sea. Originally a castle complex built for King Herold, the area served as a fortress for the Jewish community during the Roman takeover of 1st Century CE. Located at the very edge of the Judean Desert, the heat is incredibly intense.

This doesn't seem to matter to Ari, since his excitement to show me every single thing Israel has to offer within a matter of days suggests we explore at any cost, even if it means hiking up Masada in 90 degrees, IN SANDALS. It's been three days of nonstop activity, and I am absolutely dead. Every minute with him is accounted for: Dead Sea, Masada, museum, Jerusalem, the Wailing Wall, steak dinner, nightclub, friend's house, festival, beach, pool party, etc. etc. etc. It's hard. I don't know anyone, I don't understand anyone, and I am hopelessly in lust with this guy who seems more interested in being a tour guide than my future husband. But, let me start from day 1.

Ari picks me up at the airport in his shiny new Mercedes. We hug, exchange cheek kisses, and I hop in the car with an air of casualness that takes every ounce of my being to muster. That flight experience took a lot out of me, and I am ready to unwind with a shower, fresh clothes, red lipstick, and a frosty glass of wine alongside this beautiful specimen I have waited so long to see. Unfortunately, Ari has other plans for me.

"We are going to the University first, there is a fair happening right now."

A *fair*? Visions of jumping directly into bed with my Israeli lover are quickly replaced by visions of carnival rides and screeching preteens.

"What kind of fair?"

He lays his hand on the steering wheel, and I notice his fingers are broad and strong, the knuckles defined and the skin tone a delicious golden brown. God, he is hot. Even his hands are hot.

"Oh there are games, bars, barbeques, and some live music. It will be fun. You can meet some friends there," he says.

Slightly revived by the idea of meeting his circle *(he wants to introduce me to his friends?! He must really like me!)* bits of long-lost energy begin to surface, which I willfully gather for what I naively believe will be a quick stop on our way to a romantic evening alone.

The fair is a far cry from the American-style carnival I anticipated. The crowd is interesting and cool, and good energy abounds. We drink a beer, listen to a bad Israeli singer that the crowd goes wild for, and smoke some hash. Most people here are very good-looking with defined jaws and olive skin. The women are especially striking. The majority are tall and thin with long, thick hair and graceful strides. Since his friends don't seem overly concerned with making me feel comfortable, I drift often into cultural analysis while they converse via guttural sound effects.

The overall experience is relatively lackluster, and my intensifying desire to shower and sleep clouds any interactions I successfully have. It's been a few hours too many at this place, and we finally head home. Exhaustion is hitting me hard, but I am wholeheartedly committed to rallying myself awake in order to spend even a fraction of a second more with Ari. We pull into the driveway of a beautiful, three-story home. Being Israeli, Ari still lives with his entire family from sister to father, all of whom are already asleep. We quietly creep up to the top floor, which he has entirely to himself.

"If you want to take a shower, the bathroom is here, just pull the lever to turn the water on. I'll be waiting for you," he croons in that raspy, seductive accent of his.

There is nothing more that I want to do at this exact minute than shower. Not only do I need to refresh myself and clean off the remnants of this very long day, I also desperately need a few minutes alone to recuperate.

The art of showering at a man's house is an intricate one - one must be wary of the time spent in the bathroom, not too long and not too short; makeup, if applied at all, must look as natural as possible, meaning he absolutely cannot hear you opening and closing containers of any kind, with the exception of lotion; scent is, above all, the clincher, and it cannot be perfumy nor can it be fruity. I am knocking one task off at a time with precision. My pulse is beating fiercely as I begin the final task of brushing my teeth; the clock is ticking, and it's time for my glamorous entrance.

I fluff my hair and provocatively open the door, wearing the sexiest pajamas I can pull off without looking like I recently bought them at El Corte Inglés for this very moment. He glances my way and then something else catches his attention.

Basketball?! He's watching basketball! No candles, no smooth jazz, no dimmed lights. My Israeli god is glued to the tv watching the Knicks play the Pacers, and there's another entire quarter to suffer through!

He averts his gaze from his flat screen back to me.

"Would you like a drink?" he asks.

"Um, sure, do you want to make drinks?" I see a cabinet filled with all sorts of fun liquors. Cherry vodka, chocolate Patron, Hendrick's Gin. But, then I notice a glass of water in his hand, and my heart drops into my stomach. He means something to quench my thirst, not a saucy beverage to tip off a sexy first night together.

"I only want water, but you can make anything you want," he says. Reading my desperation for something, anything to calm my nerves, he reacts. "Have you tried the Chocolate Patron? It's so good. Do you want a shot?"

A shot. Perfect!

"Yeah, why not? I've never had it before." It goes down smoothly, but doesn't loosen me up nearly as much as I hope. Drinking more, however, is out of the question. The reality that we are going to be sitting here like roommates watching sports together starts to sink in. And then, he flips the proverbial switch.

Looking directly at me, Ari starts to smile, slowly and slyly. "So, what do you want to do?" he asks.

I bite my lip a little to appear as suggestive as possible and smile back. I'm in. I've got him. He lowers his water to the table, grabs my arm, and pulls me onto his lap.

"This is good," I reply.

His lips are perfect, and he kisses me. Really slowly, intentionally. He starts off light, brushing my lips with his, then pressing my lips with his, then parting my lips with his tongue, slipping it around mine with a deep, methodical rhythm that I surrender to completely. All of my cells are on fire. I run my fingers through his thick hair, my other hand making its way over his muscular abs to the bottom of his shirt. I slip it over his head to expose his athletic build. I pass my own lips over his broad chest as his smooth hands make their own way all over my freshly-lotioned body.

With absolutely no effort at all, he picks me up and playfully tosses me onto the bed. A little voice in my head reminds me, *I am in ISRAEL!* This exotic, sexy, confusing place with this exotic, sexy, confusing man. Like a soft porn movie scene, he slowly crawls on top of me, tendrils of hair falling into his smoky eyes and arms wrapping around my lower back. He pulls me into him, my hands reaching down to tug off his jeans.

And with that, I totally succumb to hours of love-making which prove even more glorious than those I spent daydreaming about it. When I wake up at 8am, my clothes are strewn all over the floor. I turn to him, and he is also awake, smiling at me with his perfect, shining teeth. He draws me close, and his mouth closes over mine. We finally get out of bed at 10:30am and make our way to the beach.

On my last day, Ari takes me to the airport and walks me to my gate. As he waves with a big smile, my eyes start to burn. These few days in Israel have transformed me a little bit, opened me up to situations and possibilities that I'd never been subject to before. I realize that there are so many things that I just don't know, so many experiences I've never had, and there are so many different cultures and ways of living that I've never seen or thought about before. Ari has shown me a completely surreal world, where everything is new and different and confusing. It is both painful and satisfying, and I crave more.

"See you in Barcelona," he says, those sexy tendrils of hair falling into his eyes again. "See you in Barcelona, Ari!" I reply, not for a moment considering his words might be empty. I foolishly choose to believe him and head back to Spain.

5
THE ARCHITECT

"Wear those pants with this shirt and your pink heels. You look great," Jenni says.

I do look great. Turns out the Spanish lifestyle of big lunches, small dinners, fresh food and walking as the main mode of transportation work well with my body. I've lost at least ten pounds since I arrived, if not more.

"Thanks, Jenni, I'll be ready in 10 minutes."

I check Facebook one more time. No message from Ari. After my epic and life-altering visit, he has all but fallen off the face of the earth. Pre-Israel, we had almost-daily video calls. Post-Israel, I'm lucky if I get a "like" on a Facebook post. No matter. My heels are extra high tonight since we are taking a rare taxi to the disco. Jenni's hypochondria struck today, and her knee might be breaking. Walking is out of the question.

The girls meet in the kitchen for one more cigarette and glass of sangria before we make our way to the club. It's almost 1am, which means we are a bit early. The Turkish boys are checking us out and making wholly inappropriate comments that we are eating up like the silky milk chocolate bars we so often pair with cheap red wine and a pack of harsh, throat-splitting Lucky Strikes. A trifecta of true heaven.

"Why don't you guys come with us?"

Bobby's eyes sparkle at the thought, but then he reminds us, "We don't have any money. It isn't the same for us as it is for you girls, no one buys us drinks."

Point taken. We each kiss Maria goodbye and shuffle out of the house, equipped with one extra carton of sugary, red sangria for the road and plenty of cigarettes. Upon arrival we gasp at the line, which extends the length of an entire block and is ripe with scantily clad twenty somethings.

"Do we seriously have to wait in that?" I ask.

"Not if you ladies come to Catwalk instead of Shoko!" Just in the nick of time, an Argentine club promoter swings over to our group of girls. "I'll even throw in a drink on the house. Anything you want," he grins.

Seeing that every club offers one drink "on the house" as bribery for its overly expensive cover charge, his offer is far from titillating. On the other hand, we aren't usually offered our choice of beverage (*does top shelf count?*), plus we are entitled to skip the line. That's what one might call a win-win in my book. We don't bother to discuss our options; the decision is made as we mindlessly follow the promoter to the entrance of Catwalk. With an air of satisfaction, he hands over several bright blue paper bracelets that ensure passage, and then we beeline for the bar.

The dance floor is still bare, but in the upper level there are some sexy foreign girls suggestively leaning over the handrail to scope out the scene unfolding below them. Soft blue lighting cascades onto the white walls, seemingly pumping in line with the monotonous undertones of house music. We adjust ourselves against the sleek, pearly bar, which is rather small but runs adjacent to the dance floor, giving us an unparalleled people-watching angle.

"Vodka with Cola Lite, please. Make that two," says Jenni. The other girls grab beers, and we sip while analyzing before starting our rounds. Most of the girls here are wearing next to nothing, and no one is Catalán. Locals know better.

"There are no men here," notes Natasha. She's right, but we know club promoters like to pack places with as many women as possible to entice the spendy men later on.

Suddenly, I feel a hand around my wrist. "What's your name?"

Ugh, animal, I think. I turn around to face what I assume will be a sloppy, drunk Brit with red cheeks and puffy eyes. But, what I actually face is quite the opposite. I feel myself viscerally react with pleasant surprise at this very handsome specimen before me, complete with shoulder-length black hair, nearly black and almond shaped eyes, smooth cheekbones, and olive skin. *I'll give you my name and my number!*

"What's yours?" I answer.

"I'm Cris. What are you drinking?"

Ah, right to the point. Cris's voice is raspy, likely from the stream of Marlboro Reds he indulges in, a vice I will soon uncover. I detect a slight accent, a rounding of the end of each word that indicates English is not his first language. He doesn't look European, but I can't seem to place his ethnicity. Nor do I really care at this moment. I just want to ensure this night ends with plenty of free drinks and a good make-out session.

"Vodka Cola light," I reply with a bit too much zest. I make a mental note to reel it in a bit, can't look overeager. He smiles seductively, one side of his mouth curling up and showcasing the tips of his teeth.

"Be right back. Don't go anywhere." He winks, and I buckle. Then I feel another hand around my wrist, this time not so flirtatiously.

"You don't actually like him, do you?" yells Natasha into my ear. "He's Argentinian, and they're all assholes. Trust me." She is such a downer when it comes to men, and she doesn't even know if he's Argentine. Miss Know-It-All. Anyway, if I am going to make a mistake, I will happily make it with him, thank you very much.

Cris returns within minutes with my drink, which is impressive since men tend to be overlooked by the bartenders. I glance at the bar and notice that not only is the girl behind it hot, but her gaze is lingering expectantly on Cris. Question answered. A fore-shadowing, perhaps. Choosing to ignore this obvious red flag, we spend the night together, dancing and drinking much more Vodka Cola Lites than my little body should handle. When the sunrise signals our time to go, we walk out together, his arm confidently draped over my shoulders.

He lights a cigarette and inhales a thick stream of chemically-laden smoke, an act that (unfortunately) lights up all my boards. "I want to take you out. What's your phone number?" he asks.

Liking this aggressive technique, I put my number into his phone with no hesitation.

"I'll call you this week," he says.

Natasha's warning flashes through my fatigued mind. "Wait. Where are you from?"

"Argentina," he winks.

All thoughts of Ari fade away as the handsome Argentinian architect-to-be kisses my cheeks and slips into a taxi. The sun is up. I must look awful. Natasha yawns. "Don't say I didn't warn you."

Jenni smiles at me when Natasha is not looking. We share a moment, pile into a taxi, and head directly to our kitchen to have one last cigarette and a snack before we go to bed. I drift into a foggy dreamland of Argentinian Casanovas.

6
BIKRAM YOGA
& MY INTRODUCTION TO
EUROPEAN LOCKER ROOMS

For years I flirted with yoga. My mother started teaching yoga when I was a teenager, and I had practiced here and there throughout college. But it was in Barcelona that yoga truly planted its seed.

In my quest to find a studio that offered both Spanish and English language classes, I came across a hot yoga facility a few blocks off Plaza Catalunya, easily accessible by Metro. Before taking my first class, I do as we all do in the US - dress in yoga clothes before walking out the door. On my short journey to the Metro, something dawns on me. *Have I actually seen anyone outdoors in exercise clothes with the exception of cyclists or runners?* No, the answer is no. My anxiety intensifies. *Am I breaking an unwritten law here? Am I standing out like an awkward foreigner who doesn't bother to pick up on the cultural nuances of the country she is in?* Yes, the answer is yes.

My discomfort is palpable as the subway whizzes to a stop. It's too late to turn back now. The doors open, and I feel a blast of warm air, thick with the scent of humidity and body odor. Cautiously, I step onto the car and hope no one notices my cultural faux pas, making a mental note to wear jeans next time.

Upon exiting the Metro Station my pace quickens, hoping to be as inconspicuous as possible now that I feel like an outsider. "Ughhh," I say out loud when it becomes clear that I need to do the unthinkable: take out a map. Lack of orientation shows weakness, and weakness is the worst. But, there isn't enough time to worry about whether or not I am melding easily into the cultural landscape because I am lost. And so I ashamedly take out my crumpled map of Barcelona, the one I keep on hand for emergency purposes only. Within fifteen minutes I am trucking up five flights to my first Spanish yoga class.

The studio assistant leads me to the classroom. Or, more accurately, to the steam room because that is exactly what it feels like when she opens the door. A burst of hot and humid air hits my skin as the stench of sweat from non-deodorized bodies simultaneously hits my nostrils. I move through the thick air to an empty space where I can place my mat. Beads of sweat and toxins, largely composed of alcohol and nicotine, are already streaming down my face, legs and arms. *Am I supposed to take an entire class like this?* Cursing myself for not bringing a towel, I consider asking the studio assistant for a rental when my thoughts are interrupted by a piercing cry in the form of a mantra.

Everyone stands. Everyone moves to position. Everyone knows what they're doing, except me. I follow along to the best of my ability, through each and every second of physical and mental torture. As a group, we move in synchronized form through 90 minutes of repeated postures in the 105-degree room with little to no water allowed.

Leaving, however, is not an option and not because of my own will to succeed. When halfway through the class a student throws in the towel figuratively and literally, the instructor blatantly and loudly calls her out. I watch as the poor thing shrinks to the size of a mouse. There's no way I am going to be that person, not to mention I might not fully comprehend whatever Spanish insults the instructor may hurl my way.

So even though I truly detest every agonizing minute and posture, I stay. My limbs regularly slip out of alignment from the ferocious waterfall of sweat cascading from my pores. The phrase, *When will this end,* thumps through my mind on repeat until the instructor finally speaks out the glorious words we have all been waiting 90 minutes to hear.

"Last pose!"

Collectively we give it our all and then at long last collapse into savasana.

But then something happens. The thing that happens at the end of every Bikram class to every Bikram student. An undeniable surge of pride sweeps over my drenched body from fingers to toes, a distinct internal vibration unlike any other. This feeling, in fact, feels so addictive, I decide I *have* to come back!

As if wafting on pillow-like clouds, I float to the locker room. In a state of lightness and freedom, I grab my things out of my locker and scan the room before my exit, unaware that I'm about to smack directly into my second faux pas: NEVER leave a workout facility in your workout clothes, especially when they are soaked through with sweat. Not an elegant look.

Locker rooms serve a purpose beyond girlish gossip after high school gym class: to shower and dress appropriately for public ventures. Except, this facility is exactly the opposite of any gym I've been to before. Here, I am surrounded by stark naked women, some with towels on their heads, others drying their hair by the mirror while only wearing thongs. Fat women, skinny women, old women, athletic women. Some are shaved, some are not. Women with sagging breasts and others with cellulite-ridden thighs. But, *all of these women* seem comfortable. And I am not simply referring to their ability to feel at total ease in their birthday suits in a shared setting. I mean that these women are comfortable *in their own skin. Could they simply accept that bodies come in all shapes and sizes? That being skinny isn't the only qualification of beauty?*

I take a moment to look at my own body. Thick thighs, tiny waist, a pronounced backside, strong arms, slender fingers. For years I've hidden my legs, my ass, my ankles that were the source of so much shame in comparison to the tall, skinny popular girls who seemed to have no problem grabbing the attention of the popular boys. *What if I had grown up in Spain? Would my body image have been different?* The thoughts roll through my head as I take in the scene around me.

No one is seemingly judging the other. In fact, the only thing they might be judging is my inability to strip in the middle of the room like everyone else who is naked or changing or applying makeup as if in their own bathrooms. The beauty and feminine strength of this envelopes me. I vow to myself that the next class I will shower and dress here alongside these confident, strong European women.

For now, with nothing to change into, all I have to do is survive the mortifying trip back to my flat in my sweat-soaked clothes.

7

YOU WANT ME TO
WORK WHERE?

As the weeks go by, my funds begin to get danger-
ously low. Asking my parents for help is an option,
but it also feels like a personal admittance of fail-
ure. Plus I've already gotten a few sizable donations
from them, and I don't want to overdo it. And so, I
start to dedicate my mornings and evenings to job
searching, applying to every position I can find that
wants a native English speaker. I apply to so many
listings that when I finally do get a call, I have no
idea who or what it is. And frankly, I can't care.

The woman on the phone, in a friendly and calm
voice, asks if we can arrange a Skype interview. Her
vague description of the position leads me to believe

she is a recruiter. I gladly accept, still unaware of the exact job or company, but feeling encouraged by the response. Two days later, I set up my camera, arrange my hair, and nervously wait for the video call to come in.

After a few rings, a lovely, dark-haired and dark-featured Spanish woman appears on my screen. She is pretty with a bright smile, and I immediately feel much more relaxed. The woman introduces herself as Marlene from Madrid but working as a recruiter in Barcelona. She speaks English perfectly. English is one of the many languages she speaks flawlessly, which I will come to find out later.

"So tell me a little bit about yourself. I see here on your CV that you are studying Spanish in Barcelona. How did you end up here?"

I tell her the condensed story: I've wanted to live in Spain since a class trip in high school. I want to speak a second language. I want to experience a new culture. And now, I don't want to leave.

"Did you know anyone here before you came to Barcelona? Have you been here before?" I answer no and no.

"How is your Spanish?" she asks.

I hate this question. My Spanish is nowhere near where I imagine it should be at this point, but it is much better than it was months ago, and I can understand nearly everything. Speaking is getting easier every day, but there is still work to be done.

"It's good!" I answer. My voice is too high. She's definitely going to notice the overcompensation.

We continue the standard interviewing process in English, thankfully, with some chit chat about life thrown in here and there. I like her, and I think she likes me too, but as the conversation comes to a close, Marlene still hasn't fully explained the position. As if reading my mind, she speaks up.

"You must be wondering about the position I am interviewing you for."

No, no, never thought about it. "Yes, I am a little curious," I say.

"I am a recruiter for cruise companies. We look for professionals, like yourself, to fill various positions on board international cruise ships. It is especially important that we hire people who are independent, speak several languages, and have experience interacting with different cultures. The position I am looking to fill at this moment is as an International Hostess. You would be in charge of guest relations and on-board presentations for English-speaking guests."

My experience with the cruise industry is absolutely zero. I have never been on a cruise ship, I have never had the desire to go on a cruise ship, and I certainly never imagined working on a cruise ship. None of this means I wouldn't consider it now, though.

"Wow. I was not expecting you to say that. Sounds very interesting," I say.

"It is.. It is a great experience. With that being said, I am very impressed with your background. Next week, the Hiring Manager for International Hosts will be coming to Barcelona to conduct face-to-face interviews. I would love for you to speak with him. Our office is located on Passeig de Gracia, near Zara. Do you know where Zara is?"

Who doesn't? Mental note: do NOT wear anything Zara related to the interview.

Marlene gives me a time and place. She does not disclose the name of the company, but my mind is spinning so quickly with excitement and anxiety that the idea of actually asking her never even crosses it. We disconnect the Skype call under the terms that we will meet personally next week for the second interview.

I sit in my chair for a minute, looking at the painting of the blonde girl in the white dress. She is so calm, so happy. I allow this soothing image to burn itself into my mind as tranquility will be necessary to survive this next grueling week before the interview. I check the clock, and there is still another hour or two before I can call my mom.

"Jenni?" She is most likely in the kitchen, so I make my way down the painting-lined hallway. "You will never guess what the interview was for!"

8

THE FLY IN MY
COSTA BRAVA

One of the ultimate rites of passage for any true
Barcelona expat-in-training is a trip to Costa Brava,
just north of Barcelona and extending approximate-
ly 136 miles to the border of France. Costa Brava is
a magical collection of tiny historical Catalán villages sprinkled throughout a jagged coastline that
provocatively snakes along the Mediterranean Sea.
The drive is stunning with imposing cliffs and blue-
green waters that lap up against unique rock for-
mations which jut forcefully into the sea. There are
natural parks, fascinating museums, quaint villages,
and exquisite food. Costa Brava has piqued the interest of many a traveler for its beauty and beaches,

and its ties to the quirky painter, Salvador Dalí, who was born in the town of Figueres where the Dalí museum is currently located. In short, a trip through Costa Brava is an enchanting way to spend a couple of days off with an equally enchanting, and oftentimes frustrating, Argentine lover.

Cris approached me on an uneventful Monday afternoon with the idea in his usual manner: last minute and unplanned, which is exactly how I like it. With both of us distressfully broke, renting a car was out of the question, so the plan is to leave early in the morning by train and head toward Girona, stopping in a small town named Flassa after about ninety minutes, where we will continue toward the Lloret de Mar by bus for another thirty minutes. Due to his demanding school and work schedule, Cris has only one night to spare, so there is little time to waste doing anything useful like, say, booking a hotel. We agree to meet at a cafe on Las Ramblas the following morning, and from there, we'll head to the train station together.

I pack an overnight bag, agonizing over the little time I have to prepare for this lusty overnight in arguably one of the most romantic regions of Spain. Packing takes me into the wee hours of the morning. As my eyelids droop wearily from excessive over-analysis, I finally settle on all of the cute clean panties I can find, a bathing suit, a dress, tight black stretch pants and my favorite whimsical white tank top, sandals and my toiletry kit.

In what feels like five measly minutes after collapsing into bed, my alarm goes off. Face puffy in desperation for more sleep, I manage to shower, dress and vacate the apartment without disturbing my roommate Monica, avoiding any unnecessary conversation about my getaway. I want to keep it clandestine for the sheer excitement of it.

I bounce brightly into our agreed-upon café meeting spot, full of pride over my punctuality and pumped to explore a new region of Europe. I check my watch, and I'm right on time. Cris is nowhere to be seen.

Shrugging, I settle onto a stool in front of a long wooden bar to wait. Multicolored liquor bottles tile the backsplash and sparkle against the rays of Barcelona's hot morning sun. The bartenders are busy making coffees for a mixed crowd of foreigners, a few of whom are clearly suffering the after-effects of a memorable night out. My own desire for coffee is overpowering, but I decide it's rude to have one before Cris arrives, so I commit to waiting. I figure I can hold out another few minutes.

ONE HOUR LATER, as I am about to walk to the train station and visit Costa Brava by my damn self, Cris stumbles into the cafe. Disheveled and laughing, he leans over to kiss me as he slips into the stool next to mine as if nothing's wrong. As if I have not been sitting here, awkwardly, for sixty fat minutes, waiting and worrying that he is standing me up.

"I am so sorry, babe. My boss let me off so late last night and then this morning my alarm didn't go off and…"

Blah blah blah, I am not listening anymore. I don't want to hear the nonsense coming out of his beautiful mouth. I turn my head away from him, and his lips brush my neck.

"I'm sorry, baby. I will make it up to you. I promise." He nips my skin lightly with his teeth and my insides crumble.

"Get me a café con leche," I demand, pissed at myself for forgiving him so easily but knowing I do not have the capacity not to.

He orders our coffees in his melodic Argentine Spanish, and I cautiously agree to put the past behind us. Cris empties the contents of a Marlboro Red on the bar, pulls out a nugget of weed, and starts rolling a joint … in front of everyone. My eyes bulge, and he laughs.

"Baby, this is Barcelona. No one cares. Do you want me to hide it? Will it make you feel better?"

Knowing we are still on shaky ground, Cris allows me to shield his activity from the cafe patrons with a flimsy napkin.

"I found a hotel for us," he says as he grips a rolled filter lightly between his pearly white teeth.

The bartender sets our coffees down. Café con leche for me, espresso for him. I see a distinct flash of annoyance on the man's face as his eyes settle on the pile of tobacco and pot sitting on the bar. My stomach tightens.

Turning back to Cris, who is completely unaware of this exchange, I remind myself never to come to this place again and probe further about the hotel. He pulls a crumpled piece of paper out of his pocket with a name and address scribbled in black ink.

"My flatmate recommended we stay here. I just have to call when we arrive at the bus station, and someone will come to pick us up."

"Nice," I respond, taking the second to last sip of my cafe con leche. "Oh my god. Is that…?"

The words escape me as I squint to get a better look at the bottom of my coffee cup. Cris follows my gaze and then bursts out laughing. It quickly becomes an uncontrollable roar. There it is, in plain daylight: a dead fly, floating at the bottom of the coffee that I just consumed. How long has it been there? Was it drowning in anguish while I sipped, emanating its dead energy directly into the liquid going down my throat? Do I want to laugh or cry?

Cris, doubles over at this point, clasps my forearm in his hand. With the other, he hands me the freshly rolled joint for which I am now utterly grateful. So grateful that I don't even bother to leave the cafe to light it. We get high, right there in front of everyone, caffeinated and *insectified*, and walk out hand in hand toward our adventure.

"How come there aren't any mountains?" I ask Cris after what seems like a very long ride.

"I don't know, it seems kind of industrial and flat, right?"

I nod in agreement, half asleep from the joint. "When are we supposed to switch again?" My zombie-like state has rendered me incapable of remembering anything of importance.

Cris suddenly sits upright. He turns sharpy to the man seated behind us and rattles off something in unintelligible Spanish. Turns back around, eyes wide. Something is obviously wrong.

"How long have we been on this train?" he asks.

I check my watch. "Two hours."

Two hours. Not a big deal, except we're going in the wrong direction. Both of us too high to notice.

"Dude, are you serious?" The train slows to a stop, and we hop off with no idea where we are or where to go. We make our way across the tracks to the northbound train where Cris starts to roll another joint while we wait. "Cris. No. Just, no."

He laughs and heeds my warning, packing the ingredients away for our eventual arrival to Lloret de Mar where we will finally have a delightful seafood dinner along the craggy Costa Brava coast. We fantasize about our destination while waiting for the train. And waiting for the train. And waiting and waiting.

It's after dark when we finally reach the bus station in Flassa. The bus we need to take is no longer running so we gather together the little cash we have to taxi the thirty minutes to our hotel since no one is answering to pick us up. Starving and anxious, this is far from the romantic escape I envisioned just a mere twenty-four hours ago.

We settle in the back of the taxi while the night sky drowns the palette of deep blues, greens and silver that Costa Brava is known for. Slightly annoyed but acutely tired, I snuggle against Cris's shoulder and gaze out the window. While the colors of the sea are invisible, the moon casts a shimmer on the waves, and a subtle but commanding outline of mountain-tops comes into view. There are sprinkles of lighted towns everywhere, making the landscape look like a clear, starry night sky. It is breathtakingly beautiful.

Cris whispers gently, "It looks like Argentina."

I respond with a surprised murmur, as it never occurred to me that Argentina might be so majestic. We sit, entranced by the scenic landscape, accentuated by brilliant lights and heady shadows, until we arrive at our hotel where, instead of initiating a lustful rendez-vous, we promptly fall asleep.

9

IS THIS AN INTERVIEW OR MANIPULATION? EITHER WAY, I'M DIGGIN IT.

Heels, I have to wear heels with this dress. It's the end of July, and it's hot as hell in Barcelona. This sun is like nothing I've felt before. Considering I'm much too broke to take a taxi and arrive looking human, I decide to leave very early, take the metro, and freshen up somewhere close by. My mind is filled with all sorts of possible outcomes to this Round 2 interview. Hell, maybe I don't even want this job. Or maybe I don't even get the job! This is only a second interview, after all. I do my best to keep an open and quiet mind during the 20-minute metro ride on the red line.

Riding the metro around noon is the best – the air conditioning is generally working, and there are little to no passengers, meaning you can relax and listen to the quiet hum of the car over the tracks. My destination is Plaza Catalunya, the polar opposite environment to what I am experiencing now.

Crowded, hot, and loud, I push my way through bands of map-toting, ice-cream devouring American and Canadian tourists and hipster Catalán teenagers skateboarding in the square. I walk toward Zara, already sweating. Inside Zara it's cool, packed with mom and daughter shopping duos who appreciate the professional look at modest prices. There is no public bathroom around, but there are both air-conditioning and mirrors, which is really what's in order.

I shamelessly clean myself up at a mirror in the back corner. Not looking half as bad as I feel is a great start. I press down the front of my light gray dress, restyle my hair, throw on some powder and a bit more lip gloss. This is as good as it's going to get. Inside my bag is a folder with some extra CVs (with the European-mandated photo on the top right corner that I was forced to take myself), a cover letter, clean paper, and a pen. Oh, and the ever-critical Spanish dictionary. You just never know when that little life-saver needs to make an appearance.

I spin away from the mirror and head toward the door, passing a mother-daughter pair.

"Nooo, mom, I like, don't know, like, the color is wrong or something…is there a pink one? Can you look? I need to go to the bathroom SO bad. Skuuuuusaaa, ooon bahn-gnoh porr fahVORR?"

There is no escape. Americans are everywhere. Sailing into the turquoise-tinted Mediterranean Sea on a cruise ship sounds more appealing every second. After reprimanding myself for judging – at least she attempted to ask for the bathroom in Spanish – I check the address of my interview for the eleventh time. Go outside, make a left, find the large brown door, and ring the third bell from the top to be buzzed in. I follow the detailed instructions and find myself walking up a large marble staircase to the third floor. The door is open, and people are fussing about, shuffling papers, making copies, speaking quickly to one another in Catalán. I stand timidly for a moment and then remind myself that this is Spain, and no one is going to offer me help unless I ask for it.

"Perdona, tengo una entrevista." My accent must be terrible. A tutor is definitely in order. While I prefer a Spanish boyfriend to tutor me, meeting real-life Spanish men in Barcelona has proven to be a very difficult task. For the time being I am happily settling for all sorts of other cultures: Turkish, Brazilian, Colombian, Middle Eastern, you get the picture. But Spanish men have not yet made an appearance in my bed, so to speak.

"For the cruise ship? Yes, go through this door and wait in the room on the left. Someone will be with you shortly."

The waiting room is very grand, with big leather couches, ornately carved wooden tables showcasing magazines in every language, and brochures of cruise ships galore. I settle on a Spanish language cruise brochure because, well, it can't hurt, and I barely get to the second page when a friendly and familiar voice pipes in behind me.

"You must be here for the interview! Hi, I'm Marlene, nice to meet you!"

Marlene is a very beautiful woman. She has a strong handshake and exudes confidence in her posture. I want to be a woman like that. Smiling, she guides me to a separate room with a long table.

"I want you to meet Mauro, the Hiring Manager of International Hosts at Mediterranean Cruises."

Mauro stands promptly, shakes my hand with a flirtatious smile and motions for me to sit down across from him at the table. He looks to be in his forties, tall and heavyset, with dark features, a shaved head, and sparkling eyes.

"Ciao, bella. Please, make yourself comfortable," he says.

Within a nanosecond I condense to dust. His voice alone is compelling enough but top it off with the elaborate gestures and overconfident smile, there is no hope of finding my backbone from this moment forward.

"You should find a new picture for your CV. You are much prettier in person."

Hook, line and sinker. For years to come I will be a shameless sucker for nearly every word that comes out of the mouths of Italian men, and it all started here.

"In my country we aren't allowed to put pictures on our resumes, so I had to take it myself," I giggle. Why did I just admit that? Mauro seems to appreciate my honesty and smiles back. He's very easy to talk to, his smooth tone enveloping and his accent charming. He has such a confident and engaging style, he could convince a new mother to leave her darling baby for a life on board, which I will come to learn happens often.

He gets to the point. He needs a native-English speaker to fill the role of hostess, present the ship and the ship's amenities to groups of English-speaking guests, handle complaints, accompany passengers on excursions to many exotic locations, attend and help facilitate cocktail parties, and just be an overall point of reference.

"It's one of the most sought-after positions on board, you know!" he says.

As a crew member, I will be expected to work every day of my contract, which could last anywhere from four, six, or eight months. I will be paid in Euro, receive free meals and housing, be provided with an allowance that can be used in the bars on board "to offer a drink to a guest," and be given the chance to explore the various ports of call including Greece, Italy, Spain, North Africa, the Baltics, and the Norwegian fjords. All of this awaits me with simply a signature of contract and some pre-embarkation training to take place in Genoa, should I be hired.

What could ever stop me from accepting this position? Truth be told, I'm not totally sure that I'm ready to leave Barcelona yet. I feel on the verge of a real breakthrough – making friends, learning the city, becoming comfortable with the language, feeling almost settled. Barcelona feels like home, and there is no place I would rather be. . .

except, maybe, Mykonos. Or Sicily. Tunisia? Never even heard of it but hell, I'll check it out. I could potentially get paid to take day trips to Rome and attend cocktail parties at night. This doesn't mean Barcelona won't be here when I get back.

Mauro sees the battle going on inside my head. The thing with these Italian men, they just always seem to say the right thing at the right time.

"Many of our itineraries stop in Barcelona, so you can still come here once a week."

Well that certainly nails it. While he hasn't officially offered me the position, I know it is mine.

"When did you need your new hires to embark?" I ask.

"In August."

August?! It's the end of July! "O-o-oh, that is, like, soon."

"Yes, darling, but first you would need to come to Italy for a week-long training and some medical exams. So in theory, it would be next week. I think you would be great for the position, so what do you say?"

No. I say no. "I just don't think I can be ready by next week," I admit.

"Well, we really need people who can embark when asked."

Manipulation. Not the last time Mauro will use this tactic. It is, however, one of the few times I stand up against it.

"I'm very sorry, but if you could push it back a few weeks, I would be more than happy to accept the job."

Mauro falls silent. Behind his twinkling eyes his mind is fast at work.

"Alright, bella. Here is what we can do. There is another training at the end of August. We will fly you to Italy to complete the training, and then you will embark right away. This gives you a couple of weeks to get everything together. Do I have a new English hostess?"

My limbs start to tingle, and my stomach engages in a series of notable backflips.

"Yes, Mauro. Yes, you do."

10
RED WINE, DARK
CHOCOLATE & CIGARETTES

"Could you pass me the sunscreen? I think I'm burning."

Our almost-daily ritual of frying together on the beach while sipping crappy sangria has turned Jenni a beautiful golden brown. That, and SPF 8 sunscreen with an added bronzing agent.

"Do you want to go in the water first? It's really hot." I'm fanning myself to no avail with a crumpled *Hello!* magazine.

"Can we go in ten minutes? I'm on the 10th song."

Jenni has quirks, many of which involve her OCD personality. She absolutely cannot move from her tanning position before completing a twelve-song rotation on her iPod, for example. Come hell or high water, that girl will not turn on her back or take a quick dip in the Med before she listens to twelve songs in their entirety. As a fellow OCD victim, I commiserate with her.

"Alright, but I really need to go in now, so I'll just meet you out there," I say.

Strolling across the long, orange-sanded beach toward the shimmering, aquamarine water, my mind drifts, as it often does, to my impending departure. Leaving Maria, Cris, Dos Rosas, this beach, daily Spanish lessons that prove more useless day by day, and parting with my sidekick Jenni, is going to be torture. We've already experienced the departure of quite a few of our closest friends in the house, including Natasha, and I have since moved to a new flat on the other side of town that was rented to me by Maria's brother. Changes have come and gone, and we learn quickly to adapt. But when the change is coming because of you and your decisions, it is even harder to swallow.

But, I'm excited. In the foggy distance of my future, I can see how significant this change will be. My life is unfolding in ways I never imagined. I threw my dreams to the universe, and the universe answered. One drastic move from my old life has created a domino effect of events. We have one life in which we can pack in as many or as few experiences as we want, and I am insatiable, so I take what comes, good, bad, and in-between. All I have to do is simply ride the wave.

Jenni plops into the water beside me. "I'm sooooo hot," she grumbles as a small wave washes over her face.

We sit in shallow water for a long time, talking about school, food, plans for the evening, and anything else we could think of to avoid the topic of departure. It's emotional for both of us. Jenni will be staying in Barcelona another two weeks after my exodus to Italy, and then she'll return to her old life.

Everyone I have met in my Spanish classes in Barcelona is adventurous and independent. Each of us has a burning passion to see the world and experience new cultures. Our concept of fulfillment is slightly more extreme than the average twenty something, but it cannot be denied that we each use travel as a means of escape. Returning means more than the bittersweet closing of a beautiful time in our lives; it also means facing the realities that we ran from in the first place, knowing none of those realities has disappeared.

Jenni's travel reasons are similar to my own in one regard. We mutually agree that we were born in the wrong country. Spain made its way into our blood and revived us. Going back means sucking out all the energy we just filled up on. This is a crisis in itself, but add a man to the picture and things get really hairy.

Jenni's man is named Frederic. He led her on only to break her heart. It's a classic story, but that doesn't make it easier. When the opportunity to come to Spain arose shortly after the relationship fell apart, Jenni was more or less on the next routine flight from

Amsterdam to Barcelona. She is not quite sure of her feelings for Frederic anymore, but she'd prefer not to find out. Unfortunately, there is no tactful way to avoid an inevitable run-in, and this fact has had her preoccupied for weeks.

"Do you want to stay in tonight? I'll come over, and we can have a red wine, chocolate and cigarette night?" she asks me curiously, as if I would ever say no!

Red wine, chocolate, and cigarettes are a surprisingly satisfying combination of things that are bad for your health but good for your emotional breakdowns. "Yes, that is exactly what I want to do. Lucia will most likely be holed up in her room talking to Giorgio like usual. I actually bought wine yesterday, but let's pick up one extra at the market just in case she joins."

Lucia, my Italian roommate, is not only sweet but also a great cook. She came to Barcelona for a parttime internship, leaving her overbearing boyfriend in Rome. Her downtime is generally spent assuring her utmost loyalty to said boyfriend by video chat, which means she never explores the day or nightlife of Barcelona.

"Or in case we need it just for us," says Jenni.

Great point. Rarely do we stop at one.

"Shall we go?" Jenni stands up in the water and makes a face at her wrinkled fingers.

"Yes, let's get going." My skin is tight and could use a lengthy break from the sun. On the short trip from the water's edge to our towels, we weave in and out of couples intensely making out on multi-colored beach towels and children running aimlessly in the sand. I pick up our empty box of red sangria and toss it in a nearby trash can, noting my slight buzz from earlier has since worn off.

"That stuff is so good but gross at the same time. Why do we keep drinking it?"

Jenni responds quickly. "Because it's cheap. Can you hold my towel for a minute while I put on my sandals?"

As I wait patiently for Jenni to slip on her gold sandals, I take in a deep breath of Barcelona air. As sad as I am to leave, the timing is actually perfect. Summer is winding down, Jenni is returning home, and my landlord will soon ask for another month of rent that I can't pay.

It's time to move on.

After my bon voyage dinner a few nights later, I sit alone in my apartment. I tear up as flashes of Don Simon sangria, tanning lotion with bronzing agent, health scares, late nights at the disco, red wine, chocolate and cigarettes race through my mind. The following afternoon I will fly to Genoa to start my training. There are so many things to be done upon my arrival, a fact I find both stressful and exciting. I feel a tingling sensation in my abdomen at the prospect of exploring a new place.

Genoa is along the Ligurian Coast, a consideration in the list of cities that Sam and I had planned to visit.

Along with the anticipation, I feel a twinge of guilt about Sam. *No, no, no. Don't think about this now.*

Pushing Sam's image out of my brain, I shuffle up the stairs and fall into bed.

PORT II
GENOA

11
AMORE A
PRIMA VISTA

Benvenuti a Italia! The hustle and bustle of the port city of Genoa is revitalizing. It lies smack in the middle of the Italian Riviera on the northwestern coast of Italy and is a major hub for the naval industry. Due to its location, Genoa has historically dominated the trade industry and today import, export, shipbuilding, finance and commerce enterprises help sustain its thriving population. Genoa is perched along the Mediterranean Sea with a range of mountains in the background, and while partly industrial, it also boasts a flattering coastline of pastel façades with green shutters and plenty of church towers extending proudly along the skyline.

The city has an energy that pulses and supports my rather cumbersome journey lugging a very weighty suitcase. The trek proves much more challenging than predicted due to that aforementioned mountain range. In an attempt to reach my hotel without a taxi, I find I must climb a variety of hills and stairs, none of which are paved. Had I known this, I would have brought everything in a backpack.

I grip the documents that carefully spell out directions to my destination as my sweaty palms smudge the important street names and numbers. After what feels like a lifetime, I arrive disheveled, arms and hands stinging from manually hauling 40lbs of personal crap on the Metro, over cobblestone streets and up a minimum of four flights of stone stairs in the blazing, late-August heat. To make matters worse, my lodging is not a hotel at all, but a shared flat hosted by an older, strict Italian couple, neither of whom speak a word of English, Spanish, or any other language I can manage, and who don't offer me water or assistance as I struggle to drag myself through the door.

I finally stumble into a room full of staring people of all ages and backgrounds. I know I look a complete mess as this has been one of my more disastrous traveling days. My scheduled layover in Milan was short, which tends to turn out badly if the incoming flight from Barcelona is late. And, because, hey, it's Spain, as predicted, the incoming flight from Barcelona was late. Upon arrival in Milan, I desperately pleaded with an airport employee to put me on a later flight to Genoa, thinking I'd surely missed my connection. But, to my amazement, my connecting flight hadn't even taken off yet.

"You maaaaayyy steeel cahtch your flight, baht you mahst rahn, I weel cawl duh attendant ata the gayt-tah."

Thankful and with mascara streaking down my face since sobbing in my window seat the entire flight from Barcelona, I ran to the gate. A beautiful, thin and impossibly long-legged Italian woman greeted me at the gate.

"Ahh, you made it! We waiting for you."

Oh my god, they held the plane for me? She started to gossip in Italian with the other attendant as I walked onto the tiniest plane I had ever flown on in my life. Akin to a Caribbean puddle jumper, I could barely squeeze myself down the aisle. My ticket indicated that yes, I have the very last seat of the vessel which means yes, I must walk by every passenger, each of whom has been held up as a result of my tardiness. Tardiness that was clearly out of my control but how would I explain that? Preparing for the worst, I swallowed my pride and braced myself for snide remarks, eye-rolling and snickers during my walk of shame to the back of the plane.

Instead, I was taken by complete surprise. Not only was I spared any negative reaction, but it seemed as if the passengers didn't even realize the plane was running late. Some were talking on cell phones, others were looking out the window, others reading the newspaper. One or two men glanced in my direction as a simple result of my being female and them being Italian men. Not one person seemed irritated or concerned. Feeling relief, I plopped down in the last seat, and before I had a chance to buckle myself in, the plane started making its way down the runway. Inhaling deeply and exhaling even more deeply, I turned and faced the window as the tiny airplane took off, bound for Genoa.

And now here I am, in the living room of a strange hotel/flat, the newest human specimen to be analyzed by what I assume is a crop of new hires. Clearly representing different corners of the European continent, each new hire has a drastically different look and demeanor. A jolly Spanish girl with curly hair and a big smile loudly welcomes me and guides me to our shared room. Marielisa will be my roommate for the five days in Genoa. She is warm and approachable, and I feel immediately comfortable in her presence. And then there is Andrew. Strikingly handsome and hailing from Sweden, with piercing blue eyes, a chiseled jaw, an ability to speak numerous languages, and a lifestyle of traveling the world, Andrew will be a role model and source of fascination to me for years to come.

There is a dinner planned for this evening for everyone to get to know one another and to go over the upcoming schedule. This gives me quite a few hours to freshen up and explore. I politely excuse myself to shower and dress. I feel reenergized by what I deem a successful arrival to Genoa (after all, I made it!), and I want to see the sights before dinner. A tiny voice in my head reminds me often, *I'm in Italy*. The epitome of romance, the jewel of the Mediterranean, the Motherland of the food I grew up eating, the birthplace of my ancestors. I allow myself to fall deeply in love at first sight with no regrets.

12
JUST CAVALLI

The training is an all-day affair. We start promptly at 9am and continue through until 6pm, with one hour for lunch. I'm fine with this, since I've already found myself in a state of strong infatuation with Fabio, an Italian kitesurfing hippie from Sardinia with long, curly hair and a tattoo behind his ear. He rolls his own cigarettes with expert precision, and unabashed-ly emanates sex. (I didn't realize at the time that 95% of Italian men have this quality, but that discovery unveils itself soon enough.)

Fabio is the first Italian man to sweep me off my feet. It starts innocently enough, each of us repeatedly catching the other's gaze from across the room until it becomes apparent that we are mutually interested.

He then boldly approaches me after class to invite me out for a drink. Our first evening out is a success, as we spend it eating pasta, drinking wine, and smoking those perfectly rolled natural cigarettes while exploring the local side of Genoa. By exploring the local side, I mean we spend hours ducking behind doors and into alleyways to make out.

There is, however, more to this trip than hot and heavy kissing sessions with dreamy Italians. I am here for a purpose and this purpose is to start a new phase of my life as an International English Host, the official onboard reference point for Americans, Brits, Australians, and any other English-speaking guests that embark. It is my duty to explain the itinerary and the ship, handle complaints, and accompany the guests on excursions. Sounds easy enough.

Only there's a kicker. Presented to us, Italian-style, at the tail end of our training with absolutely no indication that this announcement will be forthcoming, our small group is informed that "explaining the itinerary and ship" is a little more involved.

"Der is a leetle beet of pahblic speaking invol-ved. You-uh will make a power poooyynt presentation to introduce the ship-uh, excursions, and schedule to the grouppa when they embark. Some-uh-times, there are 10 guests, and some-uh-times, there are 500."

FIVE HUNDRED? I am expected to speak in front of five hundred freaking people? Until this point in my life, I've never spoken in front of a group larger than my high school Literature class. Why didn't anyone mention this before? I look around the room as everyone's mouths drop open in shock. Flabbergasted as I am, I take solace in the fact that we are all in this together. People begin to chatter and complain in various languages, the volume of our voices rising until Mauro quiets us down.

"Don't-uh wohrry, we practice, oh-kayay?"

And practice we do, for the next day and a half until everyone is successfully convinced of his or her ability to engage and sell excursions to crowds of five hundred or more. On the final day, our group finishes early and goes out for a farewell lunch in the center square. Beer and wine are flowing, but I remind myself to be cognizant of my intake.

Tonight is my last hurrah with Fabio, and I must be on my A-game. He has oh-so-romantically rented a crappy hotel room for the two of us to share our final night together to consummate our increasingly passionate and very short-lived love affair. The plan is set: we'll first go to dinner, then take a romantic stroll, and finally head back to the hotel.

And we do, only somewhere on our romantic stroll we take a wrong turn and find ourselves lost in a grittier part of town. Mutual fear has a way of strengthening any bond, and I make a mental note to use this anxiety as fuel in the bedroom.

When we finally do arrive safely at our love nest, Fabio opens a bottle of wine and rolls the two of us a cigarette. As the alcohol forms a light cloud over my brain, I let him take control of our impending coital union. I soon find myself on the bed with Fabio on top of me, grinding very slowly, kissing me softly, and playing with my hair as his own long locks entangle with mine. Never one for "gentle lovemaking," I motion for him to remove my shirt, and then my bra, and then the rest. I lie naked for a few moments as he remains fully dressed, the textured fabric of his jeans against my bare skin heightening my feelings of pleasure. I begin to undress him, stroking his perfectly muscular torso as I pull off his shirt. I reach to unbutton his jeans. As we tug them off together, I break away from his intensifying kisses to look down at the entirety of this masterful specimen I have before me.

I break into a wide smile. Laughing is out of the question so I muffle my reaction as audible satisfaction and lean in for another kiss. I look down again to double-check that my eyes do not deceive me. Nope, they do not. If only I had the wherewithal to snap a picture to keep this memory tangibly alive.

Under the curly mop, the nose ring, the chakra tattoos placed in arbitrary corners of his body, my Dazed & Confused Italian stallion is sporting black, skin-tight briefs with the words *JUST CAVALLI* written in 2-inch block letters -- block letters that are not just disproportionate to the size of the briefs themselves, but also outlined in sparkling rhinestones. Rhinestones that are literally gleaming in the reflection of soft light coming from the nightstand. Could there possibly be anything more Italian than this? For

my very first Italian experience? No, there could not.
Jackpot!
Needless to say, my night is *fantastico*.

The next morning, however, is rough. It is my very
first embarkation day and not only am I functioning
on about two hours of broken, drunken sleep, I am
now stuck in a van filled with an embarking crew
from the Philippines, who are wholly delightful but
fiercely curious. Talking is about the last thing I want
to do (running a marathon comes in a close second),
but since many of them have been on board a cruise
ship before, the insight they provide is useful.

Beneath the main deck is an entire society that
remains completely hidden to passengers. There are
living quarters, of course, but there is also a doctor's
office, a crew bar, a gym, a tailor, and a classroom. On
bigger ships, there are multiple classrooms, as well as
dining messes, offices and a reception area for crew
only. I find out that the lower ranking your position,
the lower your cabin will be situated. Not only are you
farther from sea level, but you'll also likely be sharing
the cabin with three other crew members. If you think
that's not a big deal, consider that the average size of
a crew cabin is about 120-180 sq. ft., with two small
closets, a desk and a bathroom. Moving upward in
rank means higher on deck and more liberties, like two
people per cabin for example, instead of three or four.

I, as a hostess, am one of the lucky ones. My position guarantees me just one roommate. It does not,

however, guarantee me a window. Those cabins are reserved for officers, which I soon come to find out is why everyone wants to date one.

A crew member's ranking also dictates the quality of their food. Housekeeping, restaurant staff and deckhands eat in a particular mess that is widely thought to serve the equivalent of gruel. But here again, my position is higher on the totem pole, which means the food I am served is always more than edible.

Upon arrival to the ship, we are shuffled in multiple directions, filling out papers and collecting keys, meeting superiors and deciphering schedules of meetings with just about everyone. At some point it dawns on me that, having never been on a cruise ship before in my life, this boat is absolutely massive, and I am not sure how I'm going to adapt. But, before I have a chance to question this revelation, I am pulled in yet another direction, toward my cabin.

I am now, officially, crew.

13
DON'T DRINK WATER
IN MY OFFICE

Where the hell am I? Get me out of here. I'm disembarking tomorrow.

It's pitch black, and my heart is racing. Just seconds ago, I woke up in a cold sweat, rocking back and forth on my tiny, stiff bed. I've been given the top bunk, a disadvantage I soon find out is reserved for new members, which means I cannot sit up entirely without slamming the crown of my head into the ceiling. Thick, searing panic is enveloping my head, and my chest feels like there is a 75-lb weight on it. The ship is vibrating at high frequency, and the threatening sound of crashing waves deafens my ears.

I sense my cabin mate shuffle and snore. I take this as a sign that we aren't sinking and pray she isn't privy to my meltdown. I quickly remember a breathing technique I learned in yoga which is meant to calm the autonomic nervous system and activate your rest mode. This seems apt for the moment and so I begin to breathe in and out for counts of four, until I finally drift off into a fitful sleep.

This morning I have an appointment with Diane, my trainer. Surprisingly, my black, puffy, sleepless eyes are pearls compared to her alcohol-induced bags. Diane is a heavy drinker to put it mildly. Our 10am meeting takes place at the Crew Bar where we plan our day over a 'green cappuccino.' To the layperson, this is known as a Heineken.

This routine and my naivete initially lead me to believe that everyone does this. It doesn't take long, however, to discover that, like many sailors, Diane has serious issues with inhibitors and is unable to draw a line between them and her job. On the bright side, though, I find that spending such a significant amount of time in the crew bar has some real benefits. Not only am I 'invited' for most drinks (to *invite* someone for a drink is a contextual term for *buying* someone a drink), I am also able to meet a majority of the crew in record time. I make friends quickly and easily and enjoy myself immensely in the process.

Working for these particular Italians on board, however, is a completely different story. They are so

…. *un*-American in their professional demeanor. Not efficient. Short-tempered. Manipulative. Petty. And COMPLETELY lacking in customer service. Helpful and empathetic are the very last words I would ever use to describe a shipboard Italian with half an ounce of power. In fact, management seems more interested in impressing one another than in ensuring a good time for the passengers.

Paltry, contradictory rules for those of us in the lower ranks of the ship's hierarchy seem to deliberately make life harder than it needs to be. For example, the hours for the crew doctor rarely coincide with crew breaks, and if you miss a shift to go to the doctor, you can be in pretty serious trouble unless you are, say, dying. At the same time, however, these ridiculous rules force one to be crafty so that many ideas are born under these distressing constructs.

There are also perks, of course. I cannot overstate the importance of accurately scoping out the scene as soon as one embarks, especially noting who is in charge of which department and identifying the assistants. People whose power is especially useful on board include the Bar Manager, Hotel Director, Doctor, Housekeeping Manager, the Maître d', Security Officer, and of course, the Captain. If you can't befriend them directly, then form a relationship with their closest assistant available. For some, this will be an impossible venture. However, for most of the pretty or handsome, young advisors, it is as easy as batting eyelashes and adorably stumbling through some

Italian phrases. For us women, flipping our hair back and forth a few times (if the hair is blonde, even better) can generally garner the attention of any Italian man, and life on board becomes relatively simple.

Unless, of course, you make the stupid mistake of falling in love with one of these crew members or have one of them fall in love with you. But, more on that later. For now, these relationships can help tremendously. Miss a boat drill? Flirt with the Security Officer or the Doctor. Break a rule? The Captain can bend it. The Maître d'can easily assist should you want to eat in the passenger restaurant to evade the questionable food in the crew mess. If you need something 'extra' to calm down an angry guest, a good relationship with the Hotel Director or Bar Manager is your gate to heaven. Morality takes a backseat to social survival when it comes to being at sea.

It is also important to become friendly with the servers in the bars you frequent the most. International Advisors have special privileges that are generally reserved for Officer levels, including drinking in the passenger area. The intention behind this is that we can invite guests out for a drink. The reality is that our little team of advisors can spend hours snacking on peanuts and drinking cocktails in the music lounge or sipping wine and scarfing down cheese in the wine bar.

But, beware. If the servers or bartenders do not take to you, they have the ability to make your drinking habit both difficult and expensive. It is widely accepted that crew members take advantage of each other. Despite this strange, manipulative lifestyle, it's possible and likely that one will form many genuine connections as we are, literally and figuratively, all in the same boat.

For me, understanding the ins and outs of seafaring life had to be done through ship legends, colleagues, and of course trial and error. I, for example, had no idea that greeting a superior with a "Buon giorno!" and coffee is always expected, regardless of the nature of your interaction, a lesson forced upon me swiftly and early on when I encountered my first problem with a guest.

Mr. Smith arrives at my hospitality desk shortly after check-in, livid about his cabin arrangements. A devoted cruiser, he has spent countless dollars on board our ships and is beyond insulted that he hasn't received his expected suite. I check his cabin number and, sure enough, he has been given plebeian lodging. Unsure of whom to talk to about this dilemma, I decide that my best bet is to approach my direct superior, Sofia.

I arrive at her office a bit apprehensive; it's my first time approaching her directly with an onboard issue that I cannot solve myself. Sofia is a pretty, blonde Italian woman with well-known jealousy issues and a lesser-known tendency to cheat on her husband. I knock on her door.

"Entra!" I hear a woman call out.

I enter. Not wanting to waste her time, I launch immediately into a detailed description of my client's concern.

"Hi, Sofia. I have a guest relations problem with a guest and was wondering if you could help me. The guest arrived yesterday, and he is complaining that he booked a suite but didn't receive one. His cabin is on Deck 4 so he is telling the truth, and he is a VIP..."

I begin to trail off as I can't help but notice what seem like daggers coming from Sofia's eyes. *What have I done?* I check the clock. *It isn't break time. I am definitely approaching her within regular office hours.* I turn to look behind me. No one there.

"Is...is this a bad time?" I manage to squeak out in mouse-like fashion.

Sofia's eyes transform into small slits of black and her mouth tightens. "Buon giorno," she sneers with absolute disgust.

"Buon giorno, Sofia," I respond politely and close my mouth.

"Now, sit down and tell me again the problem."

Like a robot, I lower myself to the couch in front of her desk. I take a sip of water from a bottle in my purse, wanting desperately to moisturize my now dry-as-straw throat. She rolls her eyes.

"I don't like that." She groans. "Don't drink the bottle when talking to me."

I shove the water back in my bag and shyly restate the problem, which seems light-years away from important at this point.

"I'll talk to the Hotel Director and see if there is something we can do," Sofia scoffs. I start to walk toward the door.

"And...."

My back stiffens and the hairs on my neck stand up, preparing myself for the criticism that is surely coming my way.

"Never enter your chief's office without first saying Buon giorno."

14

THE ART OF AN ITALIAN STORIA D'AMORE

Scary bosses aside, life on board is exciting. There is always something or someone to analyze. From the mental to the physical, each culture has its stereotypes, and it's a blast dissecting them.

'Guess the nationality' is a popular pastime for those of us unlucky enough to be stuck with embarkation duty, when teams of crew are forced to spend the morning or afternoon (or both!), standing along the gangplank like statues, greeting the thousands of passengers embarking for their holiday cruise. The game goes like this: If their hands are flying, they are Italian. If they wear fedora hats, they are Portuguese. If they are pale, red, and out of breath, British. Tall

and stern, German. On the verge of tears, French. Already complaining, American.

Sometimes the embarkation duty can surpass seven hours. We sneak smoke breaks every chance we get, imbibe unhealthy amounts of espresso at the bar whenever our superiors aren't looking, gossip about the most recent crew party or discuss where to get the best sandwich in tomorrow's port of call.

Though most hate it, I actually secretly enjoy the embarkation process as it takes people watching to a whole new level and gives me a chance to practice my newly acquired but rather terrible Italian. Moreover, and perhaps more importantly, embarkation duty increases the chances of meeting some of the officers as they leave and reenter the ship after a free day in port.

Oh, those officers. The majority are Italian men boasting a riveting mix of pretentiousness, sexual prowess and bold flirtatiousness. The word "officer" itself can evoke disgust and resistance along with undeniable attraction and sensual activation. There's nothing like a man in uniform and those white, fitted shirts with stripes on the shoulders give me flutters to this day. Not to mention, officers have their own cabins and access to all the finer things on board, from food to drink to drugs. No one wants to admit to being an officer-chaser, but everyone does it.

My first officer, and first real Italian boyfriend, is Fernando. We meet within days of my arrival as he is the Safety Officer in charge of the safety training course which I am forced to take solo because my schedule rendered me unable to take the required group class.

I immediately find Fernando incredibly handsome in a slightly nerdy way. His dark rimmed glasses and neatly trimmed goatee get my juices flowing instantaneously. He looks much older than his thirty-one years, but the sea will do that to you.

"Buon giorno, parli l'italiano?" He croons in his deep, melodic voice.

"No, no, only English," I smile and hope he doesn't notice the shame over my lack of language skills. Everyone on board is proficient in at least two, if not four languages, with exception given to the British dancers who form a solid clique and fraternize almost exclusively with the best-looking officers. They, like myself, only speak English.

"Okay, I try in English."

He seems nervous, which I find adorably charming. Fernando walks me around the ship, step by step, showing me the lifeboats and escape routes. I pay attention to about 5% of it, the other 95% I spend lusting over him so that when the time comes to take the exam a few days later, I fail miserably.

"Honey," Fernando cocks his head at me, my test in hand. "What happen? I show you all!" He has a wonderfully gravelly voice that melts me completely.

"I don't know, I didn't understand well I guess." I smile.

He smiles back. "Is okay. You do better the next time."

He scribbles something unintelligible on a clipboard and shoos me away before anyone else can notice that I have just been let off the hook. I venture briskly toward Sofia's office for a meeting, gliding in late, still fantasizing about my new Safety Officer crush. She immediately tosses a 40-page packet of Safety Instructions at me.

"Here. Translate this by tomorrow, it is important."

I flip through the pages.

"Um, excuse me, this is all in Italian, and I don't speak Italian."

She knows this. It's a set up. "I don't care. Find a solution. Go now, I have to meet with the Captain."

The packet seems immensely overwhelming; until it dawns on me that this is a blessing in disguise. I pull out my ship phone and scroll down to 'Safety Officer.'

"Si, pronto?"

"Ciao, Fernando, it's the English Advisor." I hear him smiling on the other end. "Sofia gave me a packet to translate from Italian, it is all the safety instructions, and it must be finished by tomorrow. Could you help me?"

A small pause.

"Of course. Come to my cabin tonight at 8, we do together."

Bingo. At 8, I knock on the door of Fernando's cabin for the first, and certainly not the last, time. To my surprise and delight, on his desk there is a gorgeous spread of canapés, chocolate covered strawberries, and champagne. We manage to translate a few pages of the packet and leave the rest for later. The rest will never be finished, nor will it ever be requested by Sofia. Funny how that works.

15
WHEN (NOT)
IN ROME

As Fernando and I fall into easy coupledom, my first contract flows along in a similar fashion. My weekly stops included Tunis, Palermo, Rome, Dubrovnik and Savona. For most of the experienced crew members, this is the itinerary from hell - mostly half day visits which don't provide enough time to leave the ship and pick up needed items, let alone explore the mysteries each stop has to offer.

I, however, am thrilled with the stops we make. Everything is new, surreal and interesting. My appetite for the unknown, from men to food to daily customs, is voracious. During the ports that I'm free, or rather, the ports where Fernando arranges for me to be free (yet another bullet point on the list of perks of dating an officer) we wander together, enjoying lunch with wine or shopping on the main promenades, holding hands and declaring our love to the world. My first contract feels like a general overview of Italian life. Fernando shows me the upside of dating an Italian; the gifts, flowers, affection and romance. It's magic.

Despite regular stops, there is one port of call that I can't seem to get to, and it's the city that I want to see the most: La Bella Roma. I am bursting to see the capital, speaking often to Fernando of the day when I will finally devour it, knowing that the day will most likely come after I disembark the ship for good. Naturally, I obsess over it. Vocally and often.

One evening, my phone rings. Fernando and I are having plates of specially-made-and-delivered pasta in his cabin as the rest of the ship munches on whatever gruel is on the menu in the crew mess. I answer quickly when I see it is my boss.

"You will be free tomorrow from embarkation duty," she says swiftly and hangs up.

I nearly recoil in confusion. Me? Free? Tomorrow? *Isn't tomorrow the day we stop in Rome?* I relay the message to Fernando, feeling anxious but wildly excited by the news.

"Ah darling, that's wonderful!" Fernando kisses me. Conveniently, he reaches into his desk drawer, pulls out an object wrapped in ribbon, and sweetly presents me with the book, *10 Things to See in Rome*.

I said life is good with an officer.

16
WILL THIS CONTRACT
EVER END?

There is one week remaining in my contract, and freedom is an utmost flavorful morsel that dances atop my tongue at all times. My plans upon disembarkation are solid – I will spend three weeks in Barcelona and then return to the good ol' USA for Christmas. My next contract is set to start some time in February, location yet to be disclosed as it is too early for Mauro to decide what my new destination will be. I prefer it this way because I can think of only two things: Spain and sleeping in without an alarm.

Dreaming aside, duty calls. I am tardy for a Gala Cocktail that I really have no interest in attending but must. There are two elegant cocktails per cruise, taking place on the first and final nights. Guests are expected to wait in an impossibly long line to enter the theater to watch a wholly uneventful introduction of the ship's management, led by the Cruise Director. It is my job, along with the team of advisors, to stand around in a pretty dress and heels, smiling broadly and waving guests on to an awful, royal blue photo back-drop that is meant to replicate the sea. Here, guests are more or less forced to take an awkward picture with the Captain, which they can later purchase for an ob-scene amount of money. Once the photo is taken, the guests are handed a complimentary glass of low-grade prosecco, at which point they can take a seat and wait until every single person in the line has taken a photo.

Women arrive in their Gala gear, the choices ranging from flattering fitted black dresses to full-on bridesmaid gowns, complete with shimmering sequins and satin shoes in which they cannot prop-erly walk. The men generally take a less forward fashion approach, arriving in suits or simply slacks and a fitted Oxford. But there are always interest-ing exceptions, like the men who choose baseball caps and sneakers for the only classy event of the entire cruise. Without fail, throughout these brutal photo sessions, anywhere from one to six gentlemen (it's always the men) will exclaim to the Captain, "If you're here, then who's up there driving the ship?!" and cackle in sheer delight at this incredibly trite and commonplace joke that he's convinced he conceived. Of course, we all chuckle in unison like puppets and guide the guest toward a comfortable seat after the puff of the flash has gone off.

I hasten my pace after checking my watch and realizing how truly late I am. Suddenly, the shrill ringtone of my ship phone pierces the air. It's the front desk calling to tell me Mauro is on the phone, and I must report to reception immediately. *That's odd*, I think to myself as both my pulse and breath quicken. Excerpts of other crew members' horror stories about last-minute contract extensions flood my mind. There is no way I am spending one extra day on this ship, let alone an entire week, or worse, a month. I have thoroughly enjoyed my first taste of ship life, but I am beyond ready to take a break and get to land for a couple of months. Fernando disembarked several weeks back, a tearful and dispiriting separation which has left me feeling lonely and checked out.

I enter the Reception office, shaking slightly. The Front Desk Manager looks at me with a sympathetic smile as she evaluates my worried, bordering-on-panic-stricken face.

"Line-uh too-ah."

I press the line and prepare myself for the worst.

"Ciao bella, come stai? Are you having a nice contract?"

Oh lord, Mauro, just get to it. We chatter for an agonizing two minutes before he cuts to the chase.

"So, my dear, what do you think about the Greek Islands?"

My heart is now pumping noticeably faster than earlier, but for a different reason entirely. "I think I would love to see them," I reply without hesitation.

"Well, there are going to be 500 Americans embarking on another ship in the Greek Islands in two weeks. The English hostess is alone, and she needs help. Do you want to go? We can transfer you next week and you will fly directly to Athens and work two cruises around the Greek Islands and Venice. Then you will be done. It's okay for you?"

It is MORE than okay for me. "Yes, of course, I will do it!" I practically scream into the phone.

"Okaaay, I will send to you the itinerary, you stahdy well the ports of call. You receive the flight details nexta weeka. Grazie mille, bella donna."

I hang up the phone. The front desk manager looks at me and brightens.

"You are happy. Where do you go now?"

"Greece," I beam. "First time."

"Ahh, Grecia. You will love. It is bellissima."

I float out of the office toward the cocktail party that I am now more than fifteen minutes late for. But, I don't care because I am going to Greece!

17
DO YOU NEED
A LIGHT?

It's 2am, and there is next to nobody in the Greek capital's airport. My driver hasn't arrived yet, and I am tired and hungry. *Why did the company have to choose the latest flight available from Rome to Athens?* To give me anxiety and keep me in a perpetual state of sleep deprivation, that's why. I fumble with the extra cigarette pack I thankfully shoved in my handbag at the last minute and wheel my two large suitcases out the door. I might as well smoke while I wait.

A burst of warm air hits my skin as the doors slide open. Outside, there is a tall, thin, very awkward looking man staring at me.

"Crew?" He asks nervously as I drop the packet back into my bag.

"Si." I reply. Oops, wrong country. How do you say "yes" in Greek?

It doesn't matter. He swiftly takes my suitcases and throws them in the trunk. I hop in the backseat, and he gets in the driver's seat. There are empty packets of cigarettes everywhere and a partially consumed bottle of Coca-Cola. I settle in as he starts to drive toward the highway.

"How long?" I ask, hoping he understands a bit of English.

"Ahhh, thirty meenoot."

We enter the freeway, and he accelerates. A lot. More than I was expecting from this rickety taxi.

"Smoke? It's okay?" I motion to him in the rearview mirror.

He proceeds to turn around completely and look at me directly, eyes wide and googly, speechlessly asking me to repeat my request as he continues to press harder on the gas pedal. We are going well over 100mph, and he is not looking at the road, but rather, at me.

"Can I smoke?" I scream loudly, clearly, and quickly, begging him with my mind to turn around and slow down.

"Ah! Yes! Okay!"

I relax a bit as he turns back around to look at the road, when before I know it, those wide eyes are staring directly into mine again.

"Light?" He is attempting to light my cigarette with his right hand, left hand on the wheel, driving at God knows what speed, as my anxiety level blows through the roof.

Then I realize something: this is out of my control. What an oddly beautiful feeling. I take the lighter, sit back in my seat, light my cigarette myself and look out the window.

"Acropolis!" My driver is pointing to a dim light on top of a hill far off in the distance.

Whether it's lit at this time of night, or it's my overactive imagination, I will never really know. What I do know is that it is during these two weeks that I nearly miss the ship for the first (and not the last) time. Talk about a loss of control.

My immediate supervisor on this contract is an extremely fit and fearless Sicilian woman named Stefanie, who immediately notices that I have a penchant for movement. Not that I have much competition as the crew on this ship is far from athletic. Stefanie invites me to do all sorts of things: join her at the gym, join her for a jog, join her for a bike ride. She's an active adventurer – if there's a mountain, she'll climb it, no matter how steep. Highways without helmets cause her no trepidation. In the few free afternoons I have on this quick contract, we manage to go as far as possible, as fast as possible, stopping only to take photos and move again. Keeping up with her is confusing, maddening, and liberating.

And then we arrived at Katakolon.

Katakolon is a port city on the Western coast of Mainland Greece. The average passenger or crew member likely wouldn't venture off the main strip chock full of touristy seafood restaurants and colorful souvenir shops. Stefanie and I, clearly, are not the average crew members, and so we ride past our colleagues on not-quite-shiny-and-new-bikes borrowed from the ship.

It starts off well. We cycle along meandering streets in town toward the pastures. Up and over hills, along the coast, past private beach coves. When we finally hit the rural side of town with its peaceful, undulating landscape of hunter green and toasted beige, it's already time to turn around.

Actually, it's past time to turn around.

Stefanie, being much more athletic than I, hits a whole new gear and flies ahead of me. Pushing as hard as I can, I suddenly hear a click. My legs are spinning but my wheels are taking me nowhere. I look down. The chain has slipped off. Not one for fixing things, I fumble for several agonizing minutes to rectify the situation. My fingers tremble and sweat is cascading from my scalp like the Seven Sister waterfalls in Norway. I look around for any sign of life to help me, realizing only then that I am smack in the middle of an empty olive grove, which could be romantic in any scenario but this one. Stefani is nowhere to be seen.

I don't have the slightest clue where I am, and Google Maps is not really an option. I'm forced to go with my directionally challenged gut, and with the chain finally back on, I begin to pedal. But where to?

I sense some movement ahead as a wave of temporary relief washes over me. I see men! Men with giant machete-looking farm tools working the land.

"Hello! Where can I find the ship?" I scream out in exasperation.

Blank stares. Of course. They don't speak English. And I speak little to no Greek.

I attempt to translate the word *ship* in every language I know before I surrender and start acting. One husky farmer, with deeply tanned skin, a scruffy beard, and sparkly eyes, lights up in recognition as my arms flail frantically in swimming and rowing motions. He waves me in the direction of the port. I thank him profusely in Greek (one of six words or phrases I thankfully memorized) and race to save my job.

The sound of the ship's horn pierces my eardrums and my stomach. I am seriously late, like later-than-the-passengers late, breaking a cardinal rule that all crew must be on board one hour before the guests. This is grounds for dismissal. I'm terrified.

Then, an idea flashes through my mind. Should I give up and stay? Learn how to cultivate olives, fall in love with a Greek man, start a life here? Appealing.

Contemplating this, I take a deep breath and continue. Over pastures, along the shore, through the town and to my fate. I turn a corner, and there she is: my floating palace. My gut fills with relief ... and dread.

I've made it. And I'll never bike with Stefania again.

18

DROWNING IN VENICE

I am free!

After two weeks sailing the Greek Islands, I am set to disembark in Venice. Since Venice, like Rome, has been a port of embarkation and disembarkation for guests, I have seen next to nothing of it during the time I've spent on board. Therefore, I have decided to forgo my company-provided flight to Barcelona to spend some days in Venice instead.

Venezia! Charming, romantic, and magical, I have no official plans except to wander aimlessly, take pictures, and sample the cuisine. Oh, and practice the basic level of Italian I have acquired through my relationship with Fernando. In fact, I am so free-to-be that I don't even have a hotel booked! The fanciful ideas have led me to overlook the logistics of staying in Venice, a wrinkle that becomes very apparent the moment I step off the gangplank and into the city.

My luggage is excessive, to say the least. Not exactly conducive to a town navigable only by foot or boat. My first obstacle is a pedestrian-only bridge that, for whatever reason, is lined with low-level stairs. Who builds bridges like that? Italians, that's who. I manage to lug my two large suitcases and three handbags over to the other side, while simultaneously fending off gypsies offering to assist for a small fee. A small fee normally turns out to be the value of whatever is inside your suitcase, since these tricksters are known to take off running with your stuff.

Sweating profusely, I realize that my adventure has only just begun. I don't know the first thing about Venice, and all I have is a map and a lot of cash to help me figure it out. I also have the sinking realization that I am getting absolutely nowhere on foot. A water taxi is the only option to make it to any hotel.

Dragging those two suitcases onto a water taxi is, to this day, one of the biggest accomplishments of my life. I manage to spill onto a seat where I catch my breath and enjoy the breezy ride. The stop with the most appealing name is where I decide to get off.

After heaving my things onto the dock (as other riders around me stare at my lack of street-smarts, none of whom bothers to help a damsel in distress), I start walking, promising myself that the first hotel

I see is the hotel I will book. Best Western. Okay, the second hotel I see. A charming little boutique hotel on a small square comes into view, and I dart inside. The lobby is rather austere considering the hotel's outer charm. My eyes settle on a middle-aged woman with a stern face and droopy eyes behind a dark wooden desk. I inquire about a single room with my questionable Italian. The rate is of zero importance to me at the moment.

"We have a room available, how many nights?" The receptionist answers me unenthusiastically in a monotone English, clicking feverishly on the keyboard. Feeling a bit defeated, I remind myself that there is plenty of time to practice my language skills in the next few days.

"Two nights, please." I sign some paperwork, leave a copy of my passport, and sprint down the hall to my room. I unload my heavy bags onto the bed and floor, barely glancing at my surroundings. Night has fallen, and I am more than ready for wine, pasta, a gelato, and bed.

Suddenly, it hits me like a load of bricks - I'm free! No time schedules, no guests, no ship phone, no boat drills, no cocktails, no obligations except to myself! I jump in the shower, dress in layers, and hurriedly take a picture of myself in the mirror. After all, this is a monumental occasion. Even though I have been traveling alone for almost a year now, this feels different. Mature. It is the first time I've ever intentionally treated myself to a "vacation." Here I am, alone in

Venice, with absolutely no plan or expectations except to eat well and walk everywhere.

An involuntary squeal escapes my lips, the only sound effect that can convey my absolute happiness. I grab my purse, take some euros from a large wad of cash equal to my salary from months on board, and run down the hall and out the door, into the glittering lights and windy streets of this charming Italian city.

Venice is dazzling. Even in the rain, the romance permeates your veins and guides you through each winding alleyway and over every glistening canal. The colors are bright, even at night. Lights are a soft golden color, and the energy is high, yet tranquil. Souvenir shop owners are aggressive and extremely flirtatious, willing to say or do anything to get you to buy a colorful and sparkling Venetian mask, which I consider but politely decline. Vendors call out to you over pizza counters, claiming the best pizza in the city. Pastries fill the shelves inside glass counters, sprinkled with powdered sugar or drizzled with chocolate. Oversized containers of Nutella adorn the shelves of nearly every panino shop, as it is a staple in Italian life and a surefire way to entice more customers.

Venetian men are particularly rugged and alternative, boasting tattoos and sexy, scruffy faces. Each building, each gondola, and every square holds an intriguing history. It is a city to explore in depth, a city to get lost in, which proves easy since maps are impossible to follow, and signage consists mostly of homemade, spray-painted arrows on walls.

My few days in Venice fuel my search for independence and self-discovery. On the final night, I repack my bags feeling fully satisfied with my decision to disembark here. And now, it is time to return to Barcelona. But, of course, not without one more snag.

It's 5am and I am, again, cursing myself for the sheer weight of my luggage as I roll it out of the hotel, over cobblestones toward the water taxi station. The hotel receptionist has cautioned me that the tide will be high early this morning, but not really having the faintest clue what he meant, I politely thanked him for the warning. Now, in the pre-dawn darkness, I can clearly see exactly what he meant.

Despite the early hour, there are several people walking around, all men in thigh-high rubber boots. I ponder the message these boots might be sending - are they fishermen? Boat mechanics? Something doesn't add up, as their attire doesn't match either scenario. I feel a pit forming at the base of my abdomen as I continue to roll my suitcases over the dampened streets.

I arrive at what I remember to be the water taxi station, only it looks different. There is now a 4-foot high platform over which I must climb to retrieve the taxi. This platform is meant to serve as a bridge over the high tide. It must have been constructed in the middle of the night. I close my eyes for a minute, considering my possibilities. I can skip the flight, wait till the tide changes, go to the airport and see if there is another flight available later today. Only I can't because I know full well that there is only one flight to Barcelona today, and that is the flight on which I'm booked.

The magnitude of my upcoming journey weighs heavily on me. Not only will I be hoisting this luggage up and down various platforms of shoddy construction, but I will also have to face the bridge with the low-level stairs that I mastered on the way here. Then, I will have to navigate the city's train station, buy the appropriate ticket, and fling this mess onto a train headed to the airport. I feel my eyes sting. *Am I crying?*

Indeed, I am. Crying like a baby, standing in front of a platform, the tide rising even more, and then I feel something. A drop. Not a tear. Not a tear of mine anyway, but a tear from … the sky. *Is it raining?*

Oh, this can't be real. What have I gotten myself into? Knowing full well I am on the verge of a total breakdown, I somehow pull myself together. Pull up the bootstraps, as they say. My mind and body go directly into survival mode, and boy, am I grateful for it. Like a robot, I throw my heavy bags onto the platform, walk to the station, wait for the water taxi, lug the cases on and off the taxi, roll them over the pedestrian bridge as I fend off the "helpers," bolt into the train station, buy a ticket, haul my luggage onto the train, arrive at the airport, board my flight, and I arrive, in one solid piece, in beautiful Barcelona.

19

THERE ARE NO FAT
PEOPLE IN EUROPE?

My mother is sobbing as I walk closer to her. Frank, my stepdad, is close behind. He's holding a colorful bouquet of flowers. It's been almost a year since I've seen my family, and only now has it dawned on me, the magnitude of my return. It is the first time that we've been apart for this long.

"Mom, come on! Why are you crying?" I laugh at her and reach out for a hug. She's so small in my arms. It feels good to hug her again. We break away, and I kiss Frank on the cheek. "Thanks, they're beautiful! I've never gotten flowers at the airport before!"

Frank, the gentleman that he is, immediately reaches for my bags and leads the way to the car.

Mom is still crying, her tiny shoulders bobbing in time with her audible inhales.

"Everyone is fat!" I whisper loudly to her, culturally shocked by the quantity of obese bodies shuffling past me.

"What, there are no fat people in Europe?" she jokes.

"There are. Usually they're American tourists," I laugh a bit pretentiously as we enter the parking garage.

There's still another 90-minute drive ahead of us to Mom and Frank's house, and my mother asks if I would like to stop in the city for dinner. A pang of something shoots through my stomach, combining feelings of excitement, guilt, and curiosity at the mention of "the city."

Sam is just an arm's length away here. We've kept in contact for nearly all of my adventure abroad, but no decision has been made as to whether or not we will reunite in person.

"Honestly, I'd prefer to go right home."

Home. I hesitated before saying that word, and I will consistently hesitate before saying it for the next several years. Where is my home? My anchor for the last months has been Barcelona. After one week in that metropolis, I felt grounded and safe, a feeling I hadn't truly experienced independently before. Now that I'm back in the US, I'm confused about how I really feel being here.

"I thought you'd be tired anyway, so I have some things prepped for dinner, lots of vegetables, and Frank can make tuna on the grill."

Vegetables, tuna?! I am in heaven. It's a rare occasion when I can eat clean and healthy on the ship, and my body has been in turmoil over the amount of oil, sugar, and carbs I regularly ingest. My mother's cooking is the only cure as it is healthy, plentiful, and delicious. And most importantly, it is always accompanied by wine and dessert.

For the next hour and change, my mother and I chat nonstop. There is no time for breathing, only talking. Poor Frank's ears are probably bleeding, but neither of us can stop. The chatter continues through dinner and two bottles of wine until I can't lift my eyelids anymore. I go to bed drunk and happy.

For the next few weeks, I shuffle around from my mom's to my dad's, to the city, and back. It isn't right away that Sam and I decide to meet in person. In fact, he makes me really work for it. It takes days of my whining and crying to see him for him to finally relent. We agree to meet at a restaurant on the square.

It's freezing. I have a sweater dress on, with thick black tights and high black boots. My black peacoat, purchased in Palermo, Sicily, on a shopping expedition with Fernando, is a warm, cozy, and guilty reminder that I do, still, sort of, technically, have another relationship. Fernando and I have arranged to embark together for our next contract, and we keep in daily contact. Nonetheless, I feel worlds away from him, and the only thing on my mind is Sam.

I hustle into the packed restaurant and scan the bar for any sign of him. My hands are shaking, and it has nothing to do with the temperature. I need a drink, fast. I pause, considering downing something quickly before he arrives. Looking to the bar, I freeze.

There he is, seated in the corner. He hasn't seen me yet. I take a deep breath. My body goes from cold to fiery hot within nanoseconds. *Oh, no, am I sweating?* The mere sight of him sends me into a total internal tailspin. Cautiously, I wind my way through the crowd to approach him. His attention shifts toward me as I shuffle closer, and we lock eyes.

My heart stops when we look at each other. My beautiful, handsome Sam; so striking, with dark hair and features, smooth skin, and strong hands. He looks sharp and mature in a long, gray peacoat and fitted jeans.

"New jacket?" I slide into the empty space next to him.

"Ye-Yeah." He stutters back.

He's nervous. I'm nervous. We hug awkwardly, and I sit down on the bar stool beside him.

"What are you drinking?" I ask, already knowing the answer. Beer for him, wine for me.

"So. What's, uh, what's up?" His voice is husky and low.

Involuntarily, I laugh. "This is a lot more awkward than I was expecting," I state.

"Way to make it even more awkward," he fires back at me.

The ice breaks. We sink into a sort of familiarity and start to talk. Small talk, safe talk. Sam catches me up on his friends, his job, and I tell him about my reunions with my parents. Our chatter becomes more animated and deeper, each very careful not to allow the conversation to wander into dangerous territory. Meaning, any talk of Barcelona or my life onboard is completely out of the question. In other words, almost a year of my life is not up for discussion. But we navigate, and it feels good.

We move on to another bar, and then a restaurant. With each drink we become increasingly flirtatious. It feels exactly like the beginning stages of dating; except I am with someone I already know almost everything about. I never want the night to end. Apparently, neither does Sam because we decide on a post dinner drink at an Irish pub. As I babble on over our nightcaps, Sam leans over and kisses me.

My cells ignite and blood rushes through my veins at top speed. All my love for Sam surges forward in that unexpected kiss. It's fucking magical. I sit back and stare at him for a moment. "Let's go back to your place."

With hesitation, Sam finishes the remainder of his beer in a gulp, and we stumble out the door into the crisp night, arm in arm.

From that night until I embark again, Sam and I are nearly inseparable, spending a majority of each week in one another's arms. It is beautiful and comfortable. I think I can stay like this forever.

But around February, the itch starts again. There is more of the world to see, and I have to go.

20
TUDO MUITO BEM

"OH MY GOD! BRAZIL?!?!"

Mauro emailed me my new contract, just as I was falsely convincing myself that I didn't want to embark again.

"I'm going to Rio!!!" I shriek with raw excitement as I open the new contract on my laptop. Port of Embarkation: Rio de Janeiro. It is the same ship I disembarked from months earlier in Greece. It is now in South America and will be for a full month before crossing back to Greece. I am more than happy.

There is just one small issue: Fernando.

Fernando and I have kept a long-distance, non-committal thing going. The reason I am offered

this contract is because Fernando set it up for me …
so we could be together again. This would all be fine,
except I'm not feeling very excited to see him. In fact, I
am more excited about the crop of Brazilian men that
will surely be on board and will surely be enticing.

I decide I'll cross that bridge when I get to it. My
focus now is getting my visa, packing my things, and
breaking the news to my friends, family, and Sam.
Telling my friends and family is manageable. They
seem to expect it. Telling Sam is a whole other story.

I have successfully led him to believe that we can
try things again. It's an offer I felt was truly valid until
being handed a plane ticket to Brazil. My wanderlust
is pulsating, and there is nothing I can do to quell it
except travel.

"Sam, I am only going to do this one contract,
and then I'll move back. I'm serious." This is a tall
order for me to fill, but my hands are tied. *I love Sam.
Why can't I commit to him?*

"Babe, it's six months. I can't wait six months. It's
so painful when you are away."

But somehow we convince ourselves to keep our
relationship going, no matter the distance. We suffer
through an excruciating and tearful goodbye, promising to stay in contact more often and make a real
plan for when I get back.

It feels so viable.

A day later, it's time for me to go. The time I've
spent with my friends and family has felt comfortable
and safe. Leaving them is heavy. In the hours leading

up to my flight to Rio de Janeiro I witness a variety of internal sensations, ranging from pure thrill to haunting uncertainty. I suck it up. This is my reality.

My father takes me to the airport on departure day. We pile my suitcase into the trunk before he settles into the driver's seat and me into the passenger's. The drive is long, and he's more jittery than usual, which says a lot. My father is a small, doting Italian-American drama king with a potent addiction to coffee and over-the-counter antacids. Our relationship is both tumultuous and intensely loving. He is, and always will be, my biggest life lesson. But that's for another memoir.

"Are you okay?" I ask him, even though I know he's not. Brazil is on the other side of this dreadful goodbye for me. For him, the only thing that will change is my absence. I squeeze his free hand, and he squeezes back.

We pull up to the airport, and I gather my things.

"Be careful, daughter, let me know that you arrive safely."

"I love you pops. I'll send you postcards."

We hug for a long time outside of the car. Tears well up in his eyes. Guilt and sadness are bubbling up in my throat, so I kiss his cheek one more time and lighten the mood by giving him a pat on the back.

"See you in a few months, Dad!" I try to appear cheery and spin on my heels toward the door. Making my way to the check-in desk, my melancholy subsides as I reach for my passport.

Oh. My. God.

My passport! *Where is my passport??* Full panic sweeps over me. There is no way I forgot my most vital piece of information. I sit down on a bench to rifle through my purse.

Nothing.

"Oh my god." I speak aloud. "No way. Nooo fucking way." My heart sinks into my stomach, and my chest feels ready to explode. My brain is spitting out a plethora of manipulation tactics to resort to in order to board the plane without a passport. *Is this a sign from the Universe? Am I supposed to stay home?* I consider running back out to find my father.

Instead, I breathe. In deeply through my nose, out deeply through my nose. Yoga, as I am growing to recognize more and more every day, has weaved its way into my psyche to calm me down. I do this deep breathing for a few minutes, eyes closed, calming down.

Suddenly, a vision. My passport is in my suitcase. Bottom left. I tear into my over-packed luggage and fumble around the section in the bottom left. I feel a rough, fabric covered booklet that is basically my lifeline. Angels start singing *hallelujah* in my ears. *What an absolutely stupid place to put it.*

"Well, that was horrifying." At this crucial moment I have no problem whatsoever talking to myself out loud, in public. I give a kiss to my passport and get in the back of a long, curvy line that will inevitably lead me to beautiful Brazil.

21

I'LL EXPLOIT MY
ANCESTORS FOR THAT

I'm in Rio de Janeiro, I repeat to myself continuously,
melodically. It's so surreal. It's also so hot, dusty, and
green. My imagination is on fire with plans of "tour-
isting." Before embarkation, I plan to catch a glimpse
of Sugar Loaf, check out Copacabana Beach, try some
açai, and maybe take a spin through Santa Teresa if
there's time. Rio is loud and chaotic and enticing, even
from inside the taxi, one that takes me directly from
the door of the airport to the entry of the ship.

*Wait minute, is this a joke? This is it? This is my
Bem vindo ao Brasil? A taxi ride and nada mais?*

Every crew member knows that once they step
onto the gangway, life is no longer theirs to dictate.

Free time is a limited commodity. The little we have of it is normally spent sleeping, eating, or going to the gym. The next four, eight or ten months are almost completely run by a superior and the guests on board, … in addition to an overly possessive and very jealous partner. No one crosses the ship's threshold without marginally considering making a run for it while there is still a chance.

However, curiosity always wins. Meeting the crew, checking out the officers, exploring new parts of the world, and the overall enticement of ship life seem an appropriate exchange for your freedom. So as I come upon the entryway and realize I will not be lounging on Copacabana beach today like I fantasized about for my 16-hour trip, I allow the tentacles of overwhelming curiosity to engulf me.

The sensations of a new adventure are stifled when I see Fernando smiling radiantly at me from the inside of the gangway.

"Benvenuto, mio amore!" He's beaming.

I have to admit, I am happy to see him. I run into his manly arms, and when Fernando releases me from our embrace, he hands me a packet.

"I got for you everything you need," he states proudly, "even your cabin key. And mine too because my cabin is your cabin now." He kisses me hard.

This is *THE* ultimate announcement of coupledom: the ever-coveted exchange of keys. If the man you are fucking gives you a spare key or hides his key in a secret spot in the corridor near his door for you to use at will, you are no longer fucking. You are making love, full stop. Receiving a key is simply ship code for "you are now my girlfriend."

I hesitate for a microsecond before accepting the reality that life on board is better this way.

"Thank you, baby. I'll go to the crew office and come to your cabin, *our cabin*, when I'm finished." I kiss him quickly and sprint to the crew purser's office.

Usually one of the busiest offices on board, I'm shocked to see the office completely empty. As I shuffle in, the crew purser swivels to face me.

Wow. A beautiful pair of icy blue eyes hijacks my concentration as I attempt to introduce myself as the English Hostess. The crew purser is damn hot with a wonderfully thick Napolitano accent and strong hands. Ugh, what is this ship? Valley of the Gods?

"You fill dees, and dees, and den you finish. What it is your sura-name-ah?"

I proudly state my last name, already knowing the reaction I'm going to receive.

His gorgeous eyes widen with excitement, "You are-ah Eetalian!"

My very Italian-sounding last name has started many conversations with beautiful Italian men, and I know where it's going, so I throw down my Ace. "Yes. My grandmother's family is from Napoli."

A look of pure astonishment crosses his face. But, okay, let's be real and historically accurate. The majority of Italian immigrants to the US originated from Naples or Sicily. So it's not entirely unique nor surprising to have such heritage. Regardless, Italians from Italy don't always know that, and there's no harm in exploiting my ancestors to flirt with men as handsome as this crew purser.

"*I* am from Naples!" he exclaims with gusto.

Neither is *this* surprising, as not only are most Italian-Americans Neapolitan or Sicilian, but so are most seamen. And with eyes like that, there is no doubt of his roots. I feign amazement anyway.

"You are? Wow! I hope we aren't related! (wink) What's your name?"

"Vincenzo."

Gorgeous. My favorite name as of this very moment. I calculate how often I can realistically visit this office during my contract without looking like a stalker. Not often enough.

"You must come to me every month on the 15th to pick up your paycheck. Or, you can sign up for the direct deposit, and you don't have to come here."

I almost choke at the thought. My brilliant intuition takes over.

"Can I think about it for a few days and come back here to let you know my decision?" My decision which will obviously be NO WAY, NEVER do I want direct deposit if it means I won't see YOU once a month. However, returning in a few days to "let him know my decision" buys me an extra interaction.

"SHORE, that is okay. Hey, aren't you the girl-friend of the first officer, Fernando?"

God damnit! I haven't been on the ship for *one hour*, and my relationship status is already solidified!

"Um, uh huh." I say meekly. I sign a few more papers and leave, feeling slightly discouraged.

But, it turns out, there's no need to be. A year later, Vincenzo will re-enter my life and leave a lasting impact.

22
PIZZA CON
SALMONE

Cruising South America proves very eventful. My team is close. Like, super close. We do everything together. Dinner, drinks, excursions, you name it, we roll deep. We even have pizza together on Sundays like a family. Always with *salmone*. It's during our downtime that we compare notes on our current love affairs – Adriana, my beautiful French cabinmate, is hopelessly in love with Luco, a Brazilian cabin steward. The Spanish hostess, Josefina, and the Brazilian Host, Andrea, are an inseparable couple. My relationship with Fernando fizzled within a few weeks of embarking, and I am free as a bird, just the way I want it.

South America is colorful and musical. Of course, there are many complicated layers underneath it all, but the short time I spend here reveals very little of its faults. Of all the cultures, Brazil sparks my curiosity the most. It feels very contrasting. Here is where I meet some of the happiest people but also some of the poorest. Houses are of every color imaginable, though some are ramshackle huts on stilts set in marshy bodies of water, home to mosquitos carrying every disease known to humanity. The people are friendly, jovial, and multicolored. And very, *very* sexual. I am totally enraptured by the Brazilian mentality toward sex. Nothing is taboo, and everything goes. It's animalistic and flirtatious, and I like it. A lot.

"What time are we going to the Bon Voyage party?"

I can hear the melancholic undertones of that question. Adriana, like most French, is spellbound by Brazil. She's absolutely crushed that the South American season is coming to an end, and while I am personally excited to get back to Europe, the familiarity of those ports bores her.

"Let's meet at 10:30pm at the Crew Bar for a drink, and then we can go together," I say. This gives us enough time to digest our pizza, take a nap, have a shower, and get dolled up for arguably the biggest party of the contract.

The Bon Voyage party itself is taking place on the outside deck, but everyone is at Crew Bar to pregame. I love the Crew Bar for a gamut of reasons, but seeing what people really look like without uniforms is the most entertaining aspect by far. It puts them in their societal places and gives me more perspective on their personalities. How a person dresses says a lot about their level of creativity, attention to detail, and let's face it, their class level. These nuances don't really exist when in uniform. It's like seeing a big bowl of pasta. Until you put the sauce on it, what can you really discern about the experience you're about to have?

With this in mind, I start scanning the room while Josefina talks a mile a minute about the crossing to Europe. The whole crew is going to change very shortly. Most on board now are Brazilian, as per the law. But with the end of season comes the end of their contracts. European season means European crew. The change inevitably stirs up emotions of nostalgia but also excitement to see what the new season will bring or, more accurately, who. With a new slew of crew members comes new friendships, romances, and stories.

Speaking of…who is *that*?

I see him from across the bar and inhale sharply. Why haven't I seen *him* before? The man is clearly Italian, with a chiseled jaw, sharp features, and incredibly tanned skin. The shape of his nose is strong, and his deep, black eyes are perfectly symmetrical and defined. His teeth are whiter than pearls, as white as his tightly fitted Officer uniform. He is absolutely knees-weakening gorgeous. I've never seen a man this beautiful, not in real life, anyway. Blood rushes to my pelvis, and I feel my hands go numb.

I turn to Adriana and whisper to her, "Who is he?"

She looks up and quietly responds, "Dominic. He's the First Engineer."

Jesus. He's perfect! Does it get any sexier than that? I turn my gaze back to him as one of the entertainers, a chirpy, boyish, and very cute Argentinian girl jumps into his arms and kisses him. Damn. Someone hands me a drink, and my attention returns once again to my little group of friends. The vision of the Engineer fades momentarily, but never completely. I don't see him again on this contract. He disembarks when we arrive in Europe.

But, if I knew then what I know now, I would have protected myself when I ran into him again.

But then again, maybe not.

23
HASHING IT
OUT

"Just one more round," I emptily promise Sam.

It's been a month since I arrived back in the US. Each return to my homeland is more and more detached. It just feels temporary. I have lived too much while away only to come back to everything being the same. People are getting engaged and having babies, talking about job promotions and epidurals. It's confusing when I have nothing to add to the conversation.

"Um, I went to Croatia!"

Blank stares.

I love being with my friends and my family, but there is no one in my circle who can identify with my identity crisis. *Who am I? Where do I belong? Why do I feel so much more comfortable being "me" in another country?* I miss the challenge of language barriers and communication quirks. I miss the old European ladies that brusquely shove me aside in the market to buy their tomatoes first. I miss sitting at a table with six friends, each speaking a different language but everyone understanding the story. I miss traveling because it doesn't allow my mind to wander, like it's doing right now as people around me chat about hedge funds and baseball stats.

Sam is still a huge part of my being and neither of us is finding the strength to let the other go. My decision to embark again is heartbreaking but inevitable. I am addicted to this life and can't allow anything or anyone to compromise it. Besides, the itinerary is based in the West Mediterranean, meaning a return to Barcelona. I sorely miss the city and will happily accept any chance to go back.

Without a clue about what's headed my way, I innocently roll my case aboard for what will be my longest and most difficult contract. The challenge of the next seven months will bless me with an incredible amount of knowledge about life, about people, and most importantly, about myself.

"Do you smoke?" The Spanish hostess, Maina, has a gravelly voice and foggy eyes which are clear indicators that she's high as a kite and not referring to cigarettes.

"Si, why? Got some?" My response lights her up.

"Well, I have hash, but it's almost gone. I can get more in Barcelona tomorrow. Do you want me to pick some up for you too?"

To my knowledge, I had never really smoked hashish until I arrived in Europe. Its smooth texture and earthy aftertaste hooked me on my first puff. Unlike a traditional marijuana joint, hash renders me completely social and energetically motivated. I can smoke hash before a cocktail party and chat with guests without the slightest concern of an onset of paranoia. I am completely in control of myself and joyful to boot. So yes, I definitely want Maina to pick some up for me.

"Well, do you want to smoke some now?"

According to my watch, we have a full hour before needing to be at the hospitality desk for an afternoon of grueling interaction with guests who are only there to complain about something or to ask a million questions that you've already answered in this morning's thirty-minute presentation that they didn't show up for. Thankfully, an hour on board is comparable to six on land, which means plenty of time to smoke, sleep, shower, and prep.

Maina and I shuffle into her tiny bathroom, about the size of a broom closet, to roll and light a joint. It's safer here since the vent in the ceiling is designed to suck out odor as efficiently as possible. We inhale, hold, then exhale directly into the exhaust, which is successfully reached only by climbing onto the toilet and shoving our faces to the vent.

"I knew you got high. I could tell by your personality. You can't imagine how happy I am to have someone to smoke with," Maina coughs out between puffs.

It is around this moment that we form an unbreakable bond that keeps us attached at the hip for the entire contract. The only times we physically separate are when we go to sleep and when hanging out with our contract boyfriends. Or, contract girlfriends.

"What do you think about the cruise director?" I ask her. I've been dying for feedback on Theresa, a short, blonde, intense woman who strikes me both as aloof and calculating.

"I hate her," Maina says. "I worked with her before, she's a bitch."

Awesome. I roll my eyes and take a final hit. This hash is good, and I'm flying. I check my face in the mirror and marvel at the redness of my eyes.

"Don't worry, niña, I've got eye drops. They are the best you can find." Maina hands me a bottle of neon yellow liquid, definitely full of carcinogens and chemicals that can't be safe to drop directly into your cornea. But, they work. Within 30 seconds my eyes are brighter than ever, and I feel protected. No one will know I'm high, and it's all thanks to these drops.

"Gracias, girl."

We agree to meet for an espresso before hospitality desk, and I float down the hall to my cabin.

This is how the contract starts and how it continues. This particular itinerary awards us more free time than I am used to, which I spend smoking, napping, sunning and practicing yoga. Since Maina is from Barcelona, we are afforded a steady supply of hash that we smoke twice daily at the absolute minimum, and my cigarette intake soars beyond cancerous levels. Moreover, the itinerary is relatively easy, so we aren't subject to too many early morning duties, leaving us ample time to party. And boy, do we party.

My team of hosts is phenomenal. There is no drama, no jealousy, only love amongst us. Thanks to this comradery, we manage to successfully navigate a very tricky management situation. The cruise director has decided early on that she doesn't like the women on the team, and the captain doesn't like the men. It's hard, but challenge once again breeds innovation. Each of us forms a connection with a manager from another department who can assist in times of need. My semi-flirtatious relationship with the hotel director proves very useful to calm clients feeling less than happy with their cabin category. There seems to be nothing that a free bottle of crappy prosecco can't fix.

Life continues in this predictably challenging and fun way for about a month, and then one day Maina says, "There's a new Brazilian hostess embarking soon. I know her, she's cool. Her name is Bella. She's a lesbian. She smokes a lot."

As usual, Maina and I are crammed inside her tiny bathroom with our faces to the vent. I inhale a drag of my second joint of the day. It's not even lunchtime yet.

"Oh yeah? Is she hot?" I've long been interested in a same-sex experience. My desire to try it out with a girl was compounded during my contract in Brazil, when most of the crew stared at me with mouths gaping when I admitted that no, I had never been with a girl.

"You have to try!" my favorite Brazilian barista insisted. "You can't fully appreciate a man until you know the other side."

She's right, I thought, and from that moment on I've kept my eye out for the appropriate woman to devirginize me.

"Yeah, she's hot," Maina coughed. "She is going to like you for sure. I would do it with her, but we are just good friends."

I toy with the idea as I contemplate the joint I just rolled. Maina, amongst her many notable qualities, has the uncanny skill of rolling the best joints, and she's since passed that skill down to me.

She must read my mind because she says, "You learn fast, niña, this joint is perfect."

"I'm hungry," I respond.

She is too, so we stumble out of her broom-closet bathroom, use the eye drops, and make our way down the hall to the crew mess, giggling over nothing.

24
NOT A LESBIAN, BUT I'LL DO LESBIAN THINGS

Our eyes connect simultaneously. An introduction isn't even necessary because I know it's her. Bella, the Brazilian lesbian, has embarked and is smoking a cigarette outside the hostess office.

"Hi, I am the English hostess," I say slowly, not sure of her level of English. She looks at me nervously.

"Falas ingles?" I ask. Her face drops. I scramble to recover her dignity. "Español?"

She lights up.

"Si! Hablo español."

We shake hands, and I guide her to the office. She's sweet, a little boyish, and very beautiful. Long brown hair, delicate pink lips, and extremely smooth skin. Her cheekbones are set high, accentuating her crystal blue eyes. Yup, she's the one, I think to myself. I am going to hook up with this girl.

I take her on a tour around the ship in Spanish. While my language skills leave a lot to be desired, I am thrilled to have someone to practice with. I remember that Bella likes to get high too, so I invite her to meet me at Maina's cabin. That's all it takes for us to become a tight team of three. Literally tight, as we now have to configure our seating arrangement in the cabin bathroom to include a third member. Smoking and gossiping quickly become our nighttime rituals.

"Chicas, voy a dormir," Maina announces. We've been crammed inside my bathroom for what seems like hours. My cabinmate, the Russian hostess, disembarked yesterday and no one is scheduled to move in until next week, leaving me with the cabin all to myself. We decide to smoke here this week for a change of scenery.

Bella and I are too high to move yet; she's seated on the toilet, and I'm on the floor. Maina slips out quietly, and I look at Bella, letting her know, without words, that she's welcome to stay. Since we don't fluently speak a mutual language, we have since invented our own. A healthy mix of Spanish, Italian, and Portuguese that only the two of us can really understand.

We look at each other, and I notice a change in her demeanor.

"You're beautiful," she says unexpectedly in English.

"So are you," I respond without hesitation.

"Ven aquí." She pulls me off the floor and onto her lap, straddling her waist. She slips a hand around my cheek.

Holy shit. This is it. I'm about to be bisexually devirginized!

It's a strange sensation. Her arms feel strong around me, but soft to the touch. It's so contrasting, my brain doesn't know how to integrate it. She's protective yet delicate.

"You are so beautiful," she repeats, and her lips move closer to mine.

I'm nervous; that much is clear. She leans in and kisses me. Gently at first, but with each second that passes, her kisses become more passionate, more sensual. My nerves melt away as fierce, primal feelings of attraction take their place. Bella stands up, with my legs wrapped around her waist, and puts me up against the bathroom door. I turn my gaze to the left, where I am met with a reflection of the two of us in the mirror. Me and Bella. Bella and me. I'm making out with a girl right now *and* I'm watching it. She turns her eyes to the mirror and catches mine. She smiles and playfully bites me on the cheek. I run my fingers through her long, soft hair as our exchange becomes more feverish. She opens the door and carries me to the bed.

Is this really me?

The sex with Bella is unreal in so many ways. Literally unreal to me because it's so new and different. Everything I've known of sex until now has been with men – and even though every man's body is different, the structure is the same. Having a woman in bed is confusing, contrasting, and exhilarating. The mind is conditioned to expect one thing but receives another; the stimulation increases tenfold. Bella's curves, her skin, her hair, even her voice, constantly surprise me. We move in unison, everything I want to happen, happens, without having to guide her at all. It's so feminine and lovely. When it's over, we smoke, laugh, kiss, talk, and finally fall asleep sweetly, together.

"I had sex with Bella last night."

Maina's eyes grow to the size of euro coins. "Oh my god, niña, how was it?! Congratulations!"

We're about to head to breakfast, and I have to tell her now while we're alone. She knew about my plans to devirginize my bisexuality and played an excellent supporting actress role every step of the way.

"It was incredible," I answer quickly. "So strange, tía. I couldn't believe it was happening. Super surreal."

"Do you like her? Do you think you might be a lesbian?"

I pause to think about this. While I enjoyed it immensely, I don't feel the way I do when I've slept with a man I like. I have no desire to, well, marry her. Hang out with her? For sure. Hook up again?

Definitely. But *be* with her? No.

"No chance. I don't have feelings for her in that way. I don't know, it's weird, I liked having sex with her, but she's still just a good friend to me."

Maina nodded. "Just be careful, Bella is sensible…"

"*Sensitive*. Bella is sensitive," I correct. This minor grammatical error is prevalent with romance language speakers, and it drives me crazy.

Maina then corrects herself. "SensiTIVE…and she might get real feelings for you."

This potential issue had crossed my mind, but I still can't grasp that Bella might feel something that I don't. I like men, and I want to ultimately be with a man. This was fun for me, and my respect for Bella as a friend doesn't change because we hook up. However, I have to be realistic – she ultimately *does* want to be with a woman. Our relationship could be easily misconstrued, so I have to be clear.

I decide to let things play out for a bit, and if things change, I'll talk to her. For now, I will enjoy.

"Si, tía, you're right. Let's see how it goes. How is your man, by the way?"

Maina is hopelessly in love with a lying, manipulative asshole from Argentina. While claiming to be in love with her, he has a long-term girlfriend at home *and* a new girlfriend on another ship. Yet, somehow Maina still can't admit to herself that he's bad news.

"We skyped last night. He says he has a medical condition, and he is disembarking from the ship for surgery. I don't believe him."

"Remind me again why you keep talking to him?" I'm disappointed in her weakness and angry at his insensitivity; my heart begins to beat faster.

"Because I love him, niña."

I roll my eyes. The word 'love' is interpreted so differently across cultures. As an American, I take the word very seriously. But, the rest of the world seems to throw it out there like candy. I bite my tongue and let the conversation drift onto another topic as we stroll to breakfast.

A full month passes before Bella and I decide to just be friends. The reality of a lesbian and sexual-ly-curious-but-straight female is an unsustainable one. It's hard, I'm attracted to her, and I wish I could feel what she feels. But I don't, and luckily once again, the timing of our breakup proves to be perfect.

It's a sunny and clear day when we stop at a small island off the coast of Portugal. It's a one-off port as the ship repositions itself in the Mediterranean Sea. I have the afternoon off and so spend it exploring. The breeze picks up as I make my way back to the ship, leaving me windblown and wild. In a port like this, it's incredibly rare that anyone, guest or crew, would embark. The flights are too complicated, and no one really lives here except retirees.

I am therefore caught completely off guard when I see a pair of familiar, ice-blue eyes at the entrance of the gangway.

He has already been watching me when I notice him. I feel a jolt in my body, as if an injection of caffeine has just been administered directly to my heart. It's none other than Vincenzo, the beautiful, blue-eyed Neapolitan crew purser I had met on my previous contract.

"Ciao." I initiate communication, as nonchalantly as possible. If I've learned anything about Italian men, it's to remain calm in their presence and feign that you don't care. He will be hooked on you immediately.

"Ciao, bella, how are you?" He returns my greeting exactly as I had anticipated, with trepidation and interest. He explains that the most recent crew purser fell ill and had to disembark. Vincenzo was immediately reassigned to this ship and will stay on board for 2 months. We discuss my contract, the management, the normal chit chat with flirtatious smiles thrown in as many times as we can fit them.

"We take a coffee soon, no?" he asks, sparkling blue eyes filled with hope that I will accept the invitation.

"Of course, let me know when you are free," I respond, leaving the timing open for him to make the next move. He winks. My stomach flips. I bid him goodbye and rush to Maina's cabin to tell her the news.

25

DO YOU LIKE
DOM PERIGNON?

The crew party is hot, dark, and sweaty, and I'm ready to go to bed. I place my empty beer bottle on the bar and proceed to weave in and out of a mass of dancing bodies.

"Maina, I'm leaving. See you tomorrow."

"Okay, niña, see you tomorrow."

I give her a knowing wink and leave. She'll head to bed soon too, though not alone. She has her eyes set on Lucas, a tall, funny, and handsome Italian Engineer with black rimmed glasses who, at present, has his arm around her waist.

"Buona notte," I chirp to him before easing my way out of the bar. I turn right into the stark white corridor. Fatigue sets in, and I stumble robotically toward my cabin until I am nearly plowed over by an Italian in white uniform… a crew purser!

"Vincenzo!" I glance at his hands as he's carrying several empty cups and a bottle of vodka. "Ohhh, I see, you are having a party without me?" I laugh and continue somewhat seductively walking in the direction of my cabin.

"Of *course* no, it is not a party without you," he calls out after me.

I take the stairs up to my deck. As I open the door to my cabin, I feel my phone buzz. Crew Purser? Yes. I answer the phone.

"Si?"

"I want to tell you good night, my darling, and invite you tomorrow to have a drink with me. Do you like Dom Perignon?"

Why, yes, I DO like Dom Perignon! "Yes, I like it." Can't sound overeager.

"Okay, tomorrow I call you, what time you finish?"

"Maybe 10pm."

"Me, I finish 9pm, so I call you after 22hrs, and we have a drink together in my cabin."

"Okay I will see you tomorrow then." I hang up the phone and squeal. Feeling satisfied, I change into pajamas, set my alarm, and fall into bed.

"Welcome on board everybody!" Dramatic background music blasts over the speakers. *God dammit! I told them I didn't want the stupid music.* Big smile.

"And I'll be your English-speaking hostess. I'm like your mom for this cruise!"

Everybody laughs. Laughing at this awful joke means my crowd averages at fifty years of age, and it's their second cruise. Once I know what I'm working with, I continue my speech. The ship looks like this, you can eat at these times, you must attend the safety drill, and here are some excursions for you to purchase.

What I mostly do is help the passengers understand what it's like being on a ship that's majority Italians: *You're going to absolutely hate it, but I'm here to convince you that it's all in your head!* Because a big part of my job is explaining "cultural differences" when cruising "Italian style." And there are many. But, instead of homing in on these differences, it proves more effective to instill a kind of separatism to make all non-Italians feel like they enjoy the cruise more than they actually do. I make them see that the variety of infuriating scenarios they will inevitably face is simply cultural humor (i.e., being pushed while waiting in line at the buffet *is funny*, dodging seemingly orphaned children running rampant on the outdoor decks of the ship at all hours of the night *is also funny*, the temporary deafness incurred from sitting next to an Italian family at dinner *is the funniest*).

These people aren't rude! They're just Italian, [insert laugh here]! It's you that's different!

"And so, ladies and gentlemen, I wish you a fantastic vacation and an excellent cruise on board! Arrivederci!"

An awful, Vanna-White-style melody erupts from the speakers, and I immediately run off the stage, fuming, in the direction of the sound station.

"Perché! La musica!" The anger brimming from my orifices dissipates when I see the two sound boys burst into laughter. Pranksters.

"Stronzi." But I can't help but laugh too. If this is what brings them joy, so be it. We share a chocolate, and I slip out the backstage door. Safely back in the crew area, Maina calls me.

"Where are you, niña? Want to smoke? I need to hear about last night."

Fuck, yes, I want to smoke. "I'll be there in 2 minutes."

The previous night was my first "date" with Vincenzo.

The promised bottle of Dom is instead a white wine from his region of Naples.

"I ask to my friend to take," he struggles to tell me. His English is shaky, but my patience is high. "Do you smoke?"

His delight over learning that I, too, am a pot-head, is priceless. He sits down next to me on the bed and lights a joint.

"Is it okay to smoke out here?" I am taken aback. Maina and I have gone through pains to shove our-selves into her tiny bathroom three times a day to smoke. We even have a lengthy procedure to mask the smell – a towel under the cabin door and another stuffed under the bathroom door. Then we spray copious amounts of air freshener when we are finished. And here is Vincenzo, lighting up on his bed!

"Yes, it's fine!" He communicates in a raspy and undeterred voice. His response is so confident and sexy, I choose not to remind him that as per the safety regulations, we should never iron clothes in our cabins or smoke in bed. Nagging is definitely not going to get me where I want to be tonight.

He hands me the joint and looks into my eyes. "I feel very comfortable with you," he says. "I don't worry for my English."

Admittedly, I feel very comfortable with him too. There is something easy about him. He's light, conversational, confident yet curious. Vincenzo has a fun personality, and I'm into it.

We finish the joint, and he leans in for a kiss. Aggressively. More aggressively than I expected from an Italian man, usually so smooth. Slightly disappointed, I do my best to slow him down. When my attempts are thwarted, I give in. The whole interaction is less than graceful, but I have been waiting two contracts for this, and by god, I am going to enjoy it! Chalking it up to first-time jitters, I focus on something else. I feel really, truly good around him. It's like I can say or do anything with no shame.

It's likely this level of comfort that keeps me coming back for more, long after he proves to be a complete asshole.

26

UMA AND
JOHN

"Do you like the film, Pulp Fiction?" Vincenzo is viscerally excited by the notion that I, too, might be a fan of his favorite film.

Obviously, I like it. Who doesn't?

"I like the scene where they dance. Uma Thurman and John Travolta. At the burger restaurant," he says.

As I wrack my brain to remember the details, Vincenzo pulls it up on his computer. Someone has clearly filmed the scene from their TV and uploaded it to YouTube, making the quality a bit fuzzy and also comical. Vincenzo suddenly pops up and starts imitating the moves.

His gorgeous, glassy blue eyes grow wider and wider with sheer enthusiasm, he says, "I want to make this dance with you!" He dramatically points a finger at me when he says the word "you," as if there is anyone else in the room. I'm laughing, both from his dance moves and at the idea of us stumbling around his tiny cabin as a poor man's Uma and John.

"Okay, let's learn it," I say.

Vincenzo pours us each a vodka cocktail to keep the mood light. After we clink glasses, he grabs my hand, spins me around and restarts the fuzzy YouTube video. For hours, we dance. Practicing the moves over and over again, laughing nonstop. Cocktail after cocktail, joint after joint, we become Uma and John.

Vincenzo is my best friend and my partner. I am in love.

When we finally nail it, it's well into the early hours of the morning. We collapse onto the bed and slip under the covers. Vincenzo and I fall asleep, both smiling, both wanting to be right here and nowhere else.

This wonderful sensation rapidly disintegrates into thin air. "He hasn't called me in two days." I stamp my foot on Maina's cabin floor like a child. "What the hell does he think? That he can disappear? We live on a fucking BOAT!"

I am *infuriated*. The morning after our magical dance party was a rushed one. We were both late for duty and barely had time to speak. Now two days have passed, and I haven't seen or heard one word from him. What happened? How could he flip his switch so easily?

"Call him, niña!" Maina encourages me. "He cannot treat you like this!"

It's true. I need to stand up for myself. I leave her cabin and make my way down the corridor toward the guest area. The only thing that could pseudo-distract me right now is coffee and a cigarette. But, low and behold, there's Vincenzo, walking directly toward me.

I sprint forward and grab his arm hard. He freezes.

"What happened to you? Where did you go?" My indignation is raging, and words are pouring from my mouth. "Do you think you can just disappear? There is no respect in that. If you don't want to see me anymore, act like a man and tell me that!"

Crew members start slowing down to listen. Everyone loves public ship drama, including myself. I'm just not usually the one instigating it. Vincenzo is standing in front of me, shocked at my reaction. His mouth hangs open.

"Well? Say something!" I'm getting louder. Increasingly out of control. *Am I being a crazy American?*

He starts stammering, "I, I…I have a problem with you."

We are now making a full-blown scene. Crowds of crew are idling by.

"I think of you too much, darling. It is bad for me. I am falling in love with you!"

Everything stops. My heart bursts. My mind can't help but run a mile a minute with validations. He thinks about me all the time… He's falling in love with me… I reply slowly this time. To know that he's in this turmoil is excuse enough.

"Vincenzo, why didn't you just tell me? I've been devastated without you these last two days. I thought you didn't care about me." This man, hopelessly in love with me, but compromised and unable to risk such deep feelings. Who knew a Napolitano man could have such a heart?

We embrace. As we depart, my breath slows, and my heart swells with adoration for him.

By the next day, I learn it's all bullshit.

"So he tells me he can't see me because he is falling in love with me, and he's "compromised", right? And I *believe* him. And then last night, I'm walking back to my cabin and who do I pass? Vincenzo, with a DANCER!"

Maina looks at me empathetically, but not surprised. Vincenzo's disappearance, while temporarily masked by an excuse of emotional turmoil, is actually just a sign that he's moved on.

But, I feel crazy. And why? I don't want to marry him! Even if the opportunity were there, I would never pursue something serious with him. There have been several men in my life with whom I've felt I had a potential future, but he is not one of them.

This betrayal, however, stings more than any recent other, and my mind becomes completely obsessed. I can't eat. I can't sleep. I lose significant amounts of weight. And when he does call me sporadically, I go running to his cabin.

The last night we spend together is full of detest. We both know it's over. His phone keeps ringing because the dancer is calling, and I hate him, but can't manage to leave.

After a fitful night's sleep, I wake up to the hairdryer blasting. He walks toward me in white boxer briefs, his belly chubbier that it was when we first started our affair.

"Seriously, you have to do that right now while I'm sleeping?" I mutter irritably as I pull on my clothes.

He laughs, and not in a jovial way.

"I'll call you later." The words barely escape my mouth before our eyes connect.

"Will you, really?" he asks with a smirk.

"No."

I walk out the door.

A few weeks later, Vincenzo disembarks. I happen to be outside the ship with Maina, smoking cigarettes. With his suitcase, he walks down the gangway toward his weeping dancer. He kisses her goodbye, dramatically.

I know he knows I'm here, and I know he's being animated to keep my attention on him. It works. My eyes involuntarily follow his every move. Vincenzo hops into the passenger side of a van set to transfer him to the airport. Good riddance, I think.

As the wheels start turning, he rolls down the window and leans out. Looking directly at me, he waves and calls out, "CIAOOOO!" The decibels of his goodbye drop significantly as the van gets farther and farther away, the "ow" eventually turning into a distant echo.

I turn to Maina, furrowing my brow. "Is he fucking serious?"

She's laughing uncontrollably.

The whole scene is so comical: the crying dancer, the final long and loud goodbye, my palpable irritation. I start laughing too. We head back inside the ship, and I never see him again.

A decade later, we will connect on social media. Our ugly breakup is acknowledged, and a new respect for each other emerges. Forgiveness is truly a beautiful thing.

The remainder of the contract, romantically speaking, is pretty bland. My days on board are filled with hash joints with Maina and living vicariously through her dramatic love affairs. On land, however, I enjoy myself immensely. Our itinerary includes stops in Spain, Italy, Madeira Island and Morocco. In Madeira, I try my first port wine. In Santa Cruz, Tenerife, I book my first Brazilian bikini wax. In Casablanca, I eat my first pigeon. In Marrakech, I witness my first Call to Prayer while en route from Jemaa El Fna Square to the Koutoubia Mosque.

Over loudspeakers, a beautifully chilling voice pierces through the air, and everyone falls silent. Behind the mosque's tower, the setting sun casts brilliant streaks of red and orange through the sky. Goosebumps spring up over my entire body, and my heart leaps to my throat. Few experiences are as moving and powerful as this.

I feel liberated when I finally finish this contract. After a rollercoaster of experiences, I am more than ready to take a break and reunite with Sam.

PORT III
MIAMI

27
COPENHAGEN

Remember when Sam dropped me off at the airport, crying? Now, I'm the one crying. Uncontrollably at that. I walk up to the check-in counter, shaking and checking my phone constantly for something from Sam, anything convincing me to stay.

We've broken up. Even though I spent the last few weeks feverishly looking for a job in the city where he lives, it wasn't enough. My final and desperate attempt to take back the life I once had, comfortable and monotonous, didn't fool either of us into continuing this relationship. For the last month of my vacation in the US, I worked hard to imagine life with Sam by my side, a condo in the city, maybe a dog at some point.

But, do I really want this?

No. I don't.

It's hard. Really hard. Relinquishing him to my past is just too much for me to bear. And I know, deep down, as I step into the airport security line that my decision to embark "one more time" has already sealed our fate. We will never be anything again.

I shuffle through the scanner and reluctantly make my way toward my gate, dramatic sobs constricting my throat. I slide into a chair in front of a window. Watching the planes outside transports me to another place, a European place; this temporarily dissolves my anxieties. Leaving the US for Europe is less of a location change than an identity adjustment. I get to be someone else in Italy, Spain, Norway, and Greece. I am someone stronger, independent, beautiful, and exotic.

"All passengers on Flight 4321 to Copenhagen may now proceed to Gate 42 for boarding."

That is me, and this is it. I check my phone one last time.

"Have a great contract." Sam's final message is cold.

I shut the phone off, direct my thoughts toward Scandinavia, and walk onto the plane.

The flight proves long and restless. After a transfer through the industrial outskirts of Copenhagen, I'm dropped off at a hotel, where I will stay until the ship arrives at port tomorrow. Not one to waste a moment sleeping when I could be exploring, I put on my boots and set to walk the city. It's cold, and I'm bundled in a big, comfy scarf, thick jeans, and a heavy jacket. In my purse are money, a map, chapstick, and a camera - my wandering essentials. With everything in tow, I set out on a three-mile journey to town.

Most people here are on bikes, and no one over the age of eighteen seems to wear a helmet. Everyone is tall, with pronounced eyes and strong jaws. I walk through a suburb of young families, passing handsome dads pushing fancy strollers while understatedly elegant wives follow alongside with toddlers. Everyone is classy.

Closer to the town center, the crowd starts to shift. Alternative teenagers gather in groups in the squares, drinking coca-colas and munching on sandwiches. Homes and apartment complexes make way to boutique shops and office buildings. Some shops have big names like *H&M*, others are local with names I cannot pronounce. While no one is openly smiling and friendly, no one is impolite either. It feels like an easy place.

My two goals for this evening are to visit Tivoli Gardens and to eat a smørrebrød, the typical Danish open-faced sandwich with rye bread and toppings of your choice. Both goals are easily attainable, but both prove to take me longer than expected.

Eating in another country is always an extremely long process for me. I know what I want – something traditional, in a restaurant with a good atmosphere, where I can eat alone without feeling like a loser and without anyone trying to talk to me in a language in which I can't communicate. If I can dine by a window, even better. But, more often than not, these rules I set for myself end up making my dining experience very stressful. The plan always seems doable until the time comes to actually do it. One restaurant doesn't have the right menu, the other one has too many tourists, this one doesn't have a menu in English, that one doesn't have the right seating. I continue to wander for hours, stomach growling, until I finally settle on a mediocre place out of pure starvation and then complain to myself the entire time that the restaurant I saw an hour ago would have been the better choice.

Since Copenhagen is so easy, though, I end up fairly satisfied by my dining decision. As I bite into my delicious open-faced sandwich (which reminds me of the open-faced cheese sandwiches my father always made me as a kid which were just as good if not better), I ponder my afternoon thus far. Copenhagen has been culturally stimulating, and I am mostly surprised by how tall people are. It's clean and livable, with a good transportation system and lots of activity. Most buildings are white or brown, immense in stature, and symmetrical. I like this city a lot and start fantasizing about what it would be like to live here.

Then I tug on my scarf. No, I couldn't live here. Too cold. As dusk sets in and the temperature drops even further, I make my way back to the hotel under the soft golden glow of street lamps. The three-mile walk back is crisp and haunting, though I feel totally safe. After collapsing in my hotel bed, I sleep soundly and deeply until my alarm rings.

28
I AM ABLE TO
FORM WORDS

I don't want to be here. This ship is completely disorganized. My cabin isn't ready, there's no itinerary paperwork for me to study, and there's an issue with my medical documents. A big part of me just wants to leave and go back to Sam.

But I've gotten this far, and I must see the fjords. Those gorgeous, narrow bodies of clean, glassy water that cut through Norway's glaciated valleys, decorated with lush greenery and gushing waterfalls. *National Geographic* has named the Norwegian Fjords one the world's greatest travel destinations, and there is no way I am missing out on the spectacle. With fjords in mind, I resist unleashing the temper tantrum that's creeping up my throat. I'll stick it out.

The HR Director gives me a temporary cabin on Deck A, close to the crew bar. Well, that's a good start. It's only a few nights' stay, but for these few nights I'll be alone, and it is essential for me to be alone while experiencing my now rather frequent mini meltdowns.

As I unpack my suitcase, I notice some snack bags tucked into the corner. Dried cherries and apricots, my favorite. My mother is the absolute best. I start crying.

Waiting for me on the bridge for boat drill is the new team. What inopportune timing. I throw my hair up into a bun and, with tears still in my puffy eyes, I stumble into the hall. My door slams closed, and it's loud, way louder than intended. Who cares? I think to myself as I continue to wallow in a pool of self-pity over how insanely difficult my life is right now.

Wiping my eyes, I spin around on my awful black heels and turn to face…him. The "him" of all "hims." The Engineer. The incredibly gorgeous Italian officer I spotted a year ago at the Brazilian Bon Voyage party. The one with the chiseled jaw, sharp, dark features, incredibly tanned skin. The one with the strong nose and perfectly symmetrical black eyes. The one with teeth whiter than pearls. The one with the Argentinian girlfriend. *God, if you're there, please let him be single on this ship.*

I stop dead in my tracks. My eyes grow involuntarily to the size of golf balls. His hair is black, and his skin is thick and smooth. His white Engine Room jumper is unzipped at the top, revealing the tips of his chiseled pecs and a gold chain. He is the most glorious thing I have seen in all my travels. I momentarily die.

He stares at me, blatantly.

I make a lame attempt to smile.

He winks.

Winks!! Did you know winking could be hot? Coming from a man like that, it's the sexiest thing you'll ever see. I die again and keep moving.

He watches me walk away, a fact of which I am so painfully aware I am finding it difficult to place one foot in front of the other. Somehow my body manages to get to the bridge, but my heart and mind are lost somewhere on Deck A.

Thankfully, my attention is seized by the sheer awesomeness of nature. From the bridge I am granted my first breathtaking glimpse of Scandinavia's awesome fjords. Huge masses of silvery rock topped with hunter green grass and thick clouds engulf the ship as it slowly sails through deep blue waters. Every so often, waterfalls appear and tumble down the side of the rock to splash thunderously into the sea. Purifying and stunning, this is nature at its peak. My pre-embarkation worries are quickly swallowed by the unending numbers of lakes, rivers, mountains, and fields that decorate the landscape.

Unfortunately, we will only spend another week or two in this natural heaven before making our way south to the Mediterranean. Along the way to the Med, we will stop in a few places I have never been and am simply ecstatic to see – St. Petersburg, Russia, Istanbul, Turkey, Odessa, Ukraine, and Costanza, Romania, to be precise.

It's this itinerary that I am now discussing with Betti, the gregariously delightful Spanish hostess I am becoming fast friends with. We are together in the crew bar, enjoying a nightcap, which turns into three, at the end of a long day.

"I am going to stay a bit longer," she responds when I tell her my plans to hit the sack. She has eyes for one of the Italian officers who is currently perched at the bar, and now would be a detrimental time for her to leave. I have already scanned the bar a minimum of 1,000 times, but the handsome engineer is nowhere in sight. *Does he have a girlfriend on board? Ugh.* A discernible pang stabs me in my stomach.

"Alright, hasta mañana," I say, rising from my barstool.

As I start for the door, a flash of something pink shoots past my eye. It's a shirt, a pink shirt on a dark, small, sexy…engineer!! *Holy shit, he's here!* Whatever fatigue I previously felt immediately evaporates. There is no way in *hell* I am leaving this bar now. Having walked too far through the exit to turn back around slyly, I feign a bathroom visit. In front of the mirror, I fix my hair and slap on more lipstick. My body is trembling. This is my chance.

Satisfied with my appearance, I head back inside and walk directly to the bar. I evaluate his position. He's standing to the right. If I move to the left, I'll be in plain view.

"I thought you were leaving!" says the bartender.

Oh goodness, they never pick up on anything, do they!

"Um, yeah, I just, uh, wanted some…Kit Kats!" *Kit Kats? Since when do I eat Kit Kats?* Maybe on the occasional Halloween as a youngster but since my official graduation from trick or treating I couldn't think of one single instance where I would have ingested a Kit Kat. Nonetheless, they are the first thing I lay eyes on when ordering, and now I am in possession of two since they happen to be on sale. As I hand over my crew pass, which serves not just as identification but also as payment, the bartender waves it away.

"They are paid for," he says. "The officer at the other side of the bar bought them for you."

OMG. My insides explode. I cautiously turn my head to face him. He's looking at me. He smiles and immediately works his way through the crowd in my direction, never releasing my gaze.

Everything around me ceases to exist as this man walks up to me. I know this sounds silly, but I don't care because it's true. It's like one of those slow-motion cinematic love scenes, where the man and woman fall in love at first sight, and everything in the background goes blurry. The girl usually says something perfectly flirty and catches his heart in an instant.

I, unfortunately, am NOT that girl tonight. The engineer's presence turns me into a certifiable idiot and a stuttering one at that. I somehow can't remember anything, from the time to my name.

"Ciao." His smile is slightly angled in a really sensual way, his eyes slim and cat-like, his teeth shiny and the canines pointed, like fangs.

Delicious. My body lurches in his direction. "Ciao." This is a good start, I think to myself. I am able to form words.

We attempt to talk. His English is very poor, and even though my Italian is decent at this point, my nerves won't allow me to speak it. We stumble through our conversation, me clutching those stupid Kit Kats while falling deeply into his every word. His name is Dominic, and he's thirty-one. Perfect. Napolitano. More perfect. Wearing a nice watch, he is funny, has a great smile, athletic build, a confident stance.

Betti and I spot each other across the bar. She is in full conversation with some of the animation team and winks at me when she sees the reason for my return.

It's getting too loud, so Dominic and I mutually decide to leave. He invites me to his cabin for a drink. When we enter, he turns on his little desk light and pours me a Southern Comfort with lemon soda. *Am I still shaking?* I push the notion out of my mind and watch him methodically pour a second for himself. We clink glasses. The soft gleam from the desk lamp dances on his cheek bones and casts shadows around the room. We sip at the same time, holding eye contact.

And that's that. We immediately succumb to an external force over which there is no control. Almost in unison we set our drinks back down. He grabs my waist, pulls me so close I can feel the slight bristle of his facial hair and his warm breath. Dominic kisses me so passionately that I go nearly limp with desire. But, I don't. I kiss back. Each second becomes more frantic, steamier. His lips are full and defined. I run my tongue over the top of his smooth teeth. His body is flawless, slender, and muscular, with incredibly structured thighs and perfectly rounded biceps which my hands devour as I feverishly remove the pink shirt. I couldn't have built a better man. My entire body is on fire; I can consciously feel thousands of tiny explosions underneath my skin. I'm simply dizzy over my want for him.

Somehow, I manage to end it at first base and head back to my cabin, to leave him wanting more. Somehow, I also manage to leave my uber-important crew pass, my access to absolutely everything on board with the sweet exception of my cabin, in his room.

"Oh god, this is so embarrassing," I murmur to myself as I dial his number.

He answers on the first ring. "Your crew pass. Don't worry, I am coming, what is your cabin number?"

Two minutes later he is at my door, indicating that he likely had an idea of my cabin location already. He stands before me in a white t-shirt that clings to his chest and low-rise gym shorts that accentuate his pelvic bones. *For the love of God.* I shyly take the crew pass as he leans in and kisses me.

"See you tomorrow," he whispers with a deep and raspy voice.

"See you tomorrow," I reply, shutting the door and floating to bed.

29
DOOMSDAY

My life on board quickly becomes consumed by Dominic. I think of him every waking second. When I'm not awake, he's the main character of every dream. For a while, he hides his cabin key above a fire alarm in the hallway, granting me free access whenever I please. The sheer thrill of knowing I can enter his living quarters without him present breaks me wide open. I feel so safe and so vulnerable.

After a few weeks, he presents me with a spare. *A spare key. One that is mine to keep.* Once again, the actual, tangible ship code for "You are now my girlfriend."

We spend every free minute hand in hand. We go out together on land when I'm not scheduled to work an excursion, a duty that becomes less frequent as my status as Dominic's girlfriend solidifies. We laugh and linger over boozy seafood lunches in Lisbon and frolic on the beach in Cadiz. Onboard, we spend most of our free time in bed or drinking aperol spritzes at the outside bar. I am madly in love with him. Borderline obsessed. I feel like I'll do *anything* to stay with him.

Still, these feelings come at a heavy cost. He has a son from a past relationship and is currently in a different six-year relationship with a girl from another ship who conveniently docks at the same port as ours every two weeks. She eventually finds out about us, and twice I'm forced to stay onboard in port to avoid a confrontation. I'm painfully aware that he's a complete womanizer, and on several occasions, he disappears at strange hours of the day. My mind goes wild contemplating where he's disappeared to, and yet I can't imagine letting him go.

In just three months, I've fallen completely under Dominic's spell and am absolutely dreading his inevitable disembarkation from the ship at our first stop in Naples, a city I have yet to discover.

"You don't know Napoli?" He asks, just a few days prior to his departure. His eyes are wide with delight imagining he can be the first one to show me his city.

"No! Show me, baby!"

With emotions running high we make plans to have a true Napolitano-style pizza, bakery-fresh sfogliatella, and a tour, guided by Dominic himself, through all the beautiful parts of the city. It is the only positive thing I have to hold on to, knowing he is departing the ship forever.

We talk about his visits to me when the ship stops in Naples, the possibility of his cruising for a week with me during his holiday, and then requesting our next contract together. I hold on tightly to these ideas, thinking that no matter what happens, I just want to be with him.

And then, doomsday, Dominic's disembarkation day.

He is set to leave at noon sharp. I have to be on duty for most of the morning, and he promises to call me before leaving so we can walk out together and explore Naples. In my own cabin, I've neatly prepared all the essentials for a full day out with him - on my bed lay a cute, flirty outfit, Euros, my camera, and a scarf. Since time will be of the absolute essence, my plan is to race here as soon as I receive his call to change out of my uniform and meet him at the exit.

Disembarkation duty is excruciating. As I wave goodbye to hundreds of people I will never care about nor see again, I start getting anxious about the time. I check my watch. 11:30, 11:45, 11:59. Nothing. I turn to Betti, who is on duty next to me.

"I need to make a call." I quickly leave and tuck into a quiet space.

His phone rings endlessly. He's probably already turned it into the crew purser. Without permission, I leave my position and rush down to the disembark- ation gangway. My heart is beating fast because I know something is wrong. *Is he okay? Is something delayed with his disembarkation? Or preferably, did they ask him to extend his contract at the last minute?*

Only nothing is wrong, per se. Dominic is fine. Totally fine. In fact, he's smiling! Laughing! I know this because I see him at the exit of the ship with his best friend by his side, a tall and tattooed Napolitano with a baseball cap and basketball shorts. They seem to be walking ashore together, luggage in tow.

And I'm frozen in the hallway. Is he … leaving? Without me?

At that moment, Dominic turns his head and catches my gaze. His face drops. My reaction is one I am not familiar with: I completely lose my shit.

"What are you doing? I thought you were going to call me?" My blood pressure spikes, and my face goes aflame.

He comes toward me and pulls me off to the side of the hallway, trying to calm me down. My breath is short, and my chest is heaving. A rock is forming in my throat. He attempts to wrap his arms around me, but I slip away. In his buttery Italian accent, he delivers five words I will never forget.

"I am sorry. I forgot."

Time stops. My heart sinks to my stomach and my stomach to the floor. Those stupid white hospital-style lights in the ship's interior pierce through my brain. *Forgot?* He forgot?? Not for a single second since I met Dominic have I experienced a lapse in memory of our relationship. From the first wink to the last orgasm, there isn't a moment I've forgotten. *Make this make sense.* Dismantled, I run off to my cabin without saying a word, tears stinging my eyes. Once inside, I collapse on the floor and sob.

Behind me, Dominic disembarks.

An hour later, my phone rings. I'm still on the floor. It's the French hostess, Christiane, her voice a beautiful bright light on my dark and stormy day. She convinces me to accompany her for a real Neapolitan pizza and beer.

Like a zombie, I walk through the city by her side, barely able to take in its rugged, at times unattainable, beauty. We plop down at a small pizzeria, complete with red and white checkered tablecloths. Under normal circumstances, we would have recognized immediately that it's a tourist trap due to its predictable decor, but normal this day is not. I am in no condition to analyze its worth, and I desperately need something to distract me.

The pizza tastes of cardboard, and whether that is due to its quality or my emotional state I will never know. Christiane tries her best to cheer me up. I so want to hug her, but it feels as if physical affection from anyone but Dominic will surely kill me.

After pizza, Christiane tells me she's due back at the ship early, and so she leaves me to wander alone. I eat two entire sfogliatella, a delightful pastry in the shape of a giant clam, crispy layers of dough on the outside and a lemony-almond paste filler with candied fruit peels on the inside. When drowning my sorrows in sugar doesn't work, I stumble along Via Toledo until I come upon a fabulous pair of tan suede boots in the window. My energy lifts as I try them on. They fit perfectly. Without thinking twice about the cost, I shove the appropriate amount of crumbled Euro into the hand of the cashier and walk back to the ship with a full belly, a fuller shopping bag, and a fully broken heart.

30
THERE IS A DOMINIC
HERE TO SEE YOU

The following days are torture. Robotically I man-
euver my way through excursions, presentations,
cocktails, and dinners, utterly shattered. I spend ob-
scene amounts of money on internet cards, checking
Facebook obsessively for any sign of him.

But as they say, time heals all wounds. Slowly
but surely, I start to come back to life. And what
they don't say, but should, is don't stop thinking
about him for even a second because when you do,
there he'll be.

On a random Tuesday about a month later,
the onboard DJ, a good friend of Dominic's and a
friendly contact of my own, calls me with a message.

Dominic will be coming to see me and can I make him a visitor pass with the crew purser.

Why didn't he call me to ask? My emotions dart all over the place in a completely disorganized fashion. Quickly recognizing it proves much better for my sanity not to know this information, I decide to go forward with his request.

A week later, we dock in Napoli, and I am a nervous wreck. I change my outfit one hundred times and rehearse my lines for our impending interaction one hundred more. As I stand in front of the mirror, in full blown conversation with myself (which is something I have been doing since dropping off the required paperwork to secure his visitor pass), there's a noise. Unrecognizable. Shrill. I involuntarily jump like a cat and turn toward the culprit.

It's my phone. I answer after two rings, strong and proud, and then I hear his deep voice. And I melt. He'll be at my cabin in five minutes.

A soft knock on my door signals his arrival, and I open with a trembling hand. Dominic is brown from the sun, eyes shimmering, smile as sexy as ever. As much as I want to hate him, there is no fiber in my being that can. Wasting no time, he enters my room and effortlessly hikes me up against a wall. We make out fanatically, like two lovers forced apart against their will, my heart beating wildly as he grips my face with his strong hands. Sex with Dominic now, like before, transports me to another dimension. We fall into bed, bodies quivering with desire and sweat.

We stay in my cabin all afternoon, talking about his holiday at home, my life on board. All the lines I rehearsed, right out the window.

"Dominic, can you call me this week? I want to hear your voice." I watch with helpless desperation as my power vanishes into thin air.

"Yes, baby, I call you, of course." He slips a hand around my cheek and pulls me in, brushing my lips gently with his.

I hear a click over the loudspeaker. No. No, no, no. The crackly voice of the German receptionist lodges itself deep into my eardrums.

"All visitors must proceed to the gangway for disembarkation."

My stomach knots. He has to go. Dominic dresses quickly and kisses me goodbye, a sexy, lingering one, promising to call once again. As soon as he shuts the door, tears begin to well. Do I already miss him? Maybe. Do I know his promise is empty? For sure.

Ten days and no call, as predicted. But that doesn't mean I don't suffer just the same. Every day feels longer than the last. My body feels tight, and I jump every time I hear a phone ring. I put a visitor pass in for him just in case he shows up, to surprise me and redeem himself, but with the lowest of expectations.

The morning we dock in Naples I beeline for my favorite coffee bar to chain-smoke while we enter the port. The port in Naples is very industrial, and it's hard to see the beauty of the city until you actually walk outside. I ponder this for a moment. Despite being surrounded by trash, pollution and dilapidated buildings, this place has something undeniably seductive. I want to know it, with or without him.

My phone rings. It's Security.

"Yes, there is a Dominic here to see you."

My heart leaps as my gut wrenches. A powerful woman would simply ignore this call, but at this moment I am far from a powerful woman. I smash my cigarette, smooth my skirt, and jettison downstairs. As always, his sheer presence takes my breath away. His fingers are covered with oil from fixing boats in the harbor, a visual that I find extremely arousing. I mention nothing about his lack of communication, I really don't want to hear his bullshit answer. Instead, I leap into his arms and lead him back to my cabin, where we engage in a round of desperate, mind-blowing sex before *finally* venturing out together into the city.

It's magical. We meander along the streets, hand in hand, smoking a joint on our way to meet his friends for pizza and wine. The restaurant offers a stunning view of the Bay of Naples, and I can see in his eyes how proud he is to call this home. It's mesmerizing, really. There's a soft breeze coming off the bay, which is all but glittering underneath the shining sun, and aromatic wafts of salty air tickle my nose.

After a delightfully boozy brunch, Dominic and I decide to walk back to the ship along the bay, strolling slowly as he kisses me sporadically and keeps one hand firmly on the small of my back. With the Castel dell'Ovo in our periphery and the Royal Palace in our sights, the afternoon feels mystic and romantic.

And yet, something feels off. He's here, but he's not. I'm here, but I'm also not.

My body fills with dread as we close in on the port, the little time I have left to make him fall in love with me is slipping through my fingers. He kisses me long and hard before I reenter the ship. I pathetically ask once again for a call, or a message, something to get me through the length of the next cruise. Another empty promise to contact me escapes his perfectly heart-shaped lips, and I go back on board feeling empty and dull.

Ten more days come and go, and like the week before, I am here in my favorite coffee bar, chain-smoking as we enter the port. The difference is that this time there is no call from security. Nor is there the next cruise, nor the next. Dominic never comes again; he vanishes from my life with no explanation. I feel broken and confused. "That's a Napolitano, for you," some would say. Maybe, or maybe it's just Dominic.

Years later, while working in Prague, I will have an extremely realistic dream about him. So vivid that when I wake up, I actually expect him to be there next to me. I will go about my busy day, unable to shake the reality of the dream and the way it activates me.

After work, I will decompress in my hotel room and routinely check my emails and messages. I'll open Facebook to a message from Dominic. My heart will leap out of my chest. *When did he write this? When I was dreaming about him?* Completely stunned, I will take a breath and read his words.

Just like in a movie, the message will be filled with regret, apologies, and compliments. I'm sorry, I was stupid, I want to fix it, you're beautiful. Lofty guarantees to see me again. We will make plans to meet in Miami, where I will be living at the time … I know. Am I really stupid enough to believe him? I don't know. May I do believe him or maybe I just want to live out this fantasy so badly that I'm willing to take the risk. Either way, it ends up not mattering because Dominic again, never shows.

31
AND SO IT ENDS
(OR BEGINS)

The rest of the contract is emotionally draining. I still have months to go and with Dominic's disembarkation comes a whole host of new staff. My new cruise director is a solid, functioning drunk who insists on team lunches out in every port with abundant amounts of wine and liquor. One such lunch leaves the hostesses so plastered that each and every one of us sleeps through our evening duties. Any other supervisor would have put the entire team on probation and made us pay a fine. Luckily, our director knows it's best to let it slide.

Our new captain, also a party-boy who genuinely likes us all, gives us even more leniency. Our cocktail parties are spent together with the officers in heated discussions over which is the best fish restaurant in Marmaris or pizza in Naples. We enjoy champagne and fruit after hours with our managers and even smoke hash in their bathrooms.

Life is easy and fun, but my heart isn't in it anymore. I am ready to be done with this life, to move on to something new. I've imbibed my fair share of alcohol and drugs, experienced a more than necessary number of foreign playboys, and shared my tiny living space for long enough. This contract will be my last.

But of course, as soon as you reach this sort of life-altering decision, something happens to throw you off your plans. In hindsight, you'll realize the pivot is actually meant to facilitate these very plans. But, at this moment, when I felt I couldn't spend one more day on board, I was asked to extend my contract through Christmas. Perhaps because of nostalgia or perhaps for financial reasons, maybe for both, I unenthusiastically accept the extension. The ship has to cross from Europe to the Caribbean for the winter season, and the main port of embarkation will be Miami.

Miami, the glamorous city where it all started for me. The city that gave me my first taste of foreign life. That delicious city where I met Ari, my studly Israeli lover. In many ways, a city that, to me, feels like Barcelona but is closer to my parents. And to boot, the very city where my recently relocated best friend loves to live.

So with that information, I decide to cross from East to West, knowing that not only will this be my last contract, but Miami will be my home. I will start my life anew amongst the glittering lights and turquoise waters of South Beach. I call my family to let them know that within just a few weeks, I will be Miami's newest resident.

My last day on board is surreal. Being the only American, my disembarkation process at Port of Miami is significantly faster and easier than everyone else's. No interrogations, no luggage searches. I simply show my US passport to the miserable port staff, and I am free.

Outside, the humidity smacks me in the face like a tennis racquet. Sweat pours from my temples in buckets. A taxi driver helps me drag my massive suitcase to the car and heave it inside. I plop into the leathery, slightly dewy back seat.

"Where to?" he asks in a thick Haitian accent.

"South Beach!" I say with a wide smile.

As we roll away, I turn to look at the ship. What an enormous hunk of material, containing a range of emotions so wide only one who's lived on it could ever comprehend the intensity. In three short years, I experienced more sentiment, passion, bewilderment, disappointment, confusion, and excitement than I ever had in my other years of life combined. Everything I ever wanted to see and feel and live was given to me via that ship. And yet, it couldn't be denied. It was time to let that life go.

Looking forward, I gaze ahead at the skyline of Miami, knowing that its skyscrapers, palm trees and hot sun are already taking their colorful places as details in the backdrop of my next, unforgettable adventure.

ABOUT THE AUTHOR

Bethany is a travel connoisseur, passionate writer and self-diagnosed tortilla addict. Her first book, *Wander Lust*, is a raw and sexy memoir revealing the love, heartache, self-discovery and pure joy that comes with a headfirst dive into the unknown. Bethany has worked in travel for almost 2 decades, proof that her BA in International Studies from Drexel University was a worthwhile choice. She's spent 10 chronicling her adventures for readers all over the world, more proof that pouring oneself into a hobby does, indeed, have its benefits.

Bethany's love for culture, history and tortillas was the catalyst for her 2022 relocation to Mexico City from sunny Miami. When not tapping away on her laptop or scribbling in a notebook at the park, you can find Bethany practicing yoga, taking endless photos of colorful Mexican pueblos, sampling mezcal, or walking aimlessly through the city for hours. Sign up for her newsletter, a weekly musing known as Love Letters (aweekendawayin.com/love-letters), and follow her travel advice on her website, A Weekend Away In (aweekendawayin.com).